SLOANE'S INSIDE GUIDE TO
SEX & DRUGS & ROCK 'n' ROLL

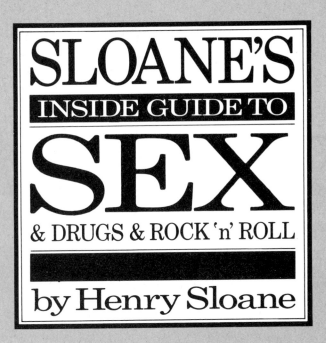

SLOANE'S
INSIDE GUIDE TO
SEX
& DRUGS & ROCK 'n' ROLL

by Henry Sloane

A PAN ORIGINAL

Pan Books   London and Sydney

First published 1985 by Pan Books Ltd,
Cavaye Place, London SW10 9PG

9 8 7 6 5 4 3 2 1

© Henry Sloane 1985
© The Sloane Zodiac by Poppé Folly 1985

ISBN 0 330 29222 6

Photoset by Parker Typesetting Service, Leicester
Printed and bound in Great Britain by
Richard Clay (The Chaucer Press) Ltd, Bungay, Suffolk

CONTENTS

'I think sex is just the most tremendous *fun!*
I spend the whole time in bed literally
roaring with laughter, and then *it* happens –
you know – and then quite soon I burst into
tears and go to sleep without saying
anything.'

INTRODUCTION

A sense of humour is awfully important.

Since the rise in structural unemployment, the emergence of the Falklands Spirit and the defeat of Arthur Scargill the Sloane population has suffered an unprecedented explosion.

The numbers entering the Sloane world, whether daughters of country peers or those of high-street bank managers, have changed the balance of British society.

The social consequences have proved dramatic in terms of misery, deprivation and a serious depletion of vital raw materials. The chronic lack of Georgian houses in Gloucestershire, with stabling, has forced new Sloanes into under-privileged living conditions – houses attached to another house, flats in Kew, commuter trains in from Dorking and Guildford, secretarial positions with paint firms.

The anxieties that this generates in the Sloane psyche cannot be over-estimated and the social consequences have been dramatic. Over the last fifteen months there has been a significant acceleration in Sloane emigration

Fresh, innocent, well-groomed debs with bare shoulders generate dangerous levels of arousal in the non-Sloane world. The gloss of the complexion promises widest possible opportunities for selective breeding.

to New Zealand and Canada, where it is widely (but erroneously) believed that the locals will not be able to tell the difference (they are stricter about the details the further from Sloane Square).

1980 – Lady Diana's hairstyle achieves recognition by the Harvard Research Press as the major influence on Britain's currency reserves.

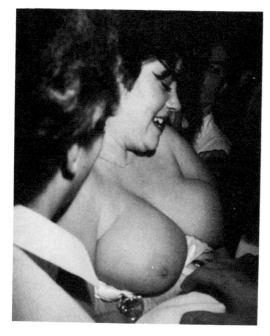

As demand for debutantes has risen, so over-supply has distorted traditional habits and manners. As the evening wears on the traditional Sloane presentation wears off.

1956 – Suez ('Johnny Gyppo's like a rat, but like a cornered rat he can be dangerous'). He was most dangerous to the Sloane population which suffered a net loss of 78 per cent over the post-Suez era.

1976 – the downward trend stabilizes as concensus politics begins to lose its grip on prevailing ideology. The question is first posed in commercial theatre: 'All right, so what's *wrong* with being middle class?'

1981 – The Royal Wedding achieves higher viewing figures in Guildford than the finals of the world snooker.

Graph showing Sloane increase in market share per 100,000 head of population

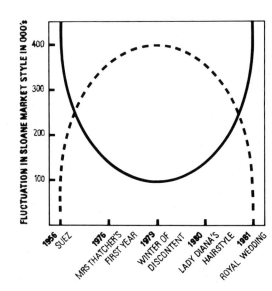

1983 – Tony Benn loses his seat. 'The Caring Society' collapses. It has become socially acceptable to have product pre-assembled in Taiwan.

(Solid line represents Sloane population, dotted line represents supply of vital raw materials – Georgian Halls, stabling, five-acre sections off the M4)

NEW SLOANE ANXIETIES

The decision to enter the Sloane world and compete with its residents is being made by increasingly under-qualified girls (see graph) without the back-up of third-generation pearls or the genuinely anal compulsions which inform the Sloane identity.

The status that has been appropriated is accordingly fragile – the highly developed accent, the mandarin vocabulary, the complex table manners all generate adrenal stress in damaging quantities.

However, the anxieties do have a positive bonding function with the rest of the Sloane world, and additionally retard the development of rogue elements in the personality – primarily, the sexual. Indeed, the Anxiety Inventory goes some way to a definition of the Sloane social presence.

THE INVENTORY

1 Falling in love with a sales director.

2 Inadvertently saying 'serviette' at a picnic ('It's what they call them on the packet, I'd had an *awful* lot to drink and I was just reading from the *packet*, honestly!').

3 Being audible in the lavatory ('It's not really on to run the taps while you're going, is it? Or is it?')

4 Introducing mother to friends ('I adore her of course, needless to say, but . . .').

5 Friends seeing photograph of parents' house ('Honestly I've no idea *why* they sold the *beautiful* rectory we grew up in – I suppose it's more *convenient*').

6 Accent slipping under stress ('Actually I was brought up in Zambia for a long time').

7 Whether to eat rice with a turned fork.

8 Ending her twenties in a semi-detached house beyond the ring road.*

*This is the most compelling anxiety, greater than fear of cancer (12 per cent), or losing the flat when Captain Markham comes back from Hong Kong (27 per cent). It was nominated by 84 per cent of all Sloanes polled and informs all Sloane endeavours. The statistics support the relevance of the anxiety, as wastage rates are increasing (22 per cent of sometime Sloanes now do live by a ring road, married to a sales director).

A Sloane hell, out by the ring road, where it is impossible to keep a nanny for more than five weeks, and Fortnum's will not deliver.

LEADING PERCENTAGE INCREASE IN ASPIRANT SLOANES

(By Father's Profession)

Ordnance officers

Bank managers

Marketing directors of pharmaceutical firms

Borough surveyors

Electrical contractors

LEADING PERCENTAGE INCREASES IN ASPIRANT SLOANES

(By Area)

Surbiton	Bedford
Guildford	Maldon
Hoddesdon	Birmingham

The social support system needed for under-privileged Sloanes is extensive. A Select Committee report recommending against Rent Support has been a step backwards, as was the discontinuation of EEC drinking vouchers. Under consideration is a government job-creation subsidy to the London auction houses to provide employment to new Sloanes arriving daily at the mainline stations throughout the capital. However, this is the age of government cuts. A further Select Committee is considering the implementation of detoxification centres to be established from Hyde Park Corner to Parson's Green, and south as far as Balham. Its effect has yet to be seen.

AUTHOR'S NOTE

Though a highly qualified social analyst I have tried to present the research material in terms that the layman will understand. This is not always possible.

A sense of humour is frightfully important, but God, really, what people will do to draw attention to themselves, even at eleven o'clock in the morning.

THE ACCENT

Now lirk! I rarely think you're foul! Nay, I mean it!
The anus is on you to behave!

Important vowel-shifts have taken place to throw non-Sloanes out of line with the orthodox movement ('ite' for 'out' has identified pseudo-Sloanes since November 1984).

Gird in bed – accomplished sexually (i.e. he giggles)

Frankly rather have a gird birk – would rather read in bed

Rarely say foul – really so foul (i.e. attractive)

Razor's awfully sharp – Rosa is clever

Blee jakes? Yuck! Rarely! – blue jokes are not amusing

No! I happen to be cheesy – I am choosy

Exclamatory Sloanes (*'Peaches!* I can't believe it!') will articulate consonants precisely; users of scheduled drugs will talk without moving their tongues. Their tongues will float in their mouths like fat fish (see *Degutantes*).

THE EXPRESSION

Oh *rarely!*

The Sloane face at rest composes itself into an expression whose function is to repel intruders*. Psychologists have identified it as a stress signal, and a pre-depressive anxiety symptom endemic to the Sloane condition. It is

*Though, 'All right doll, you're dancing with me now,' can flip the Sloane on to her back where she will lie helplessly, like a turtle (see *Rude Boys*). It will not improve her dancing, but then, nothing will.

Lady Sarah Armstrong-Jones' features fall naturally into the Sloane's public expression.

re-presented in her telephone manner where, in talking to strangers she will introduce a dead note to her delivery. According to the *Statistical Increase by Category in the Abuse of Scheduled Drugs* (H.M.S.O. 1984) it is possible that Novocain is being used for this purpose.

THE VOICE

The Sloane voice was developed in conjunction with Japanese psychological fighting systems in which precisely pitched cries demoralize an armed opponent. Sloane autopsies reveal a larynx like a cat's cradle.

The voice cannot be rendered in print, but some lessons may be learned from close attention to the audible effects of a circular saw. Three Sloanes having lunch sounds like a car crash.

THE LAUGH

The purpose of the laugh is not to invite, or to transmit data. The function of the laugh is to frighten. It is aimed at the centre of the forehead where it lands with the force of an ice pick. Semi-automatic laughter will be sprayed in two arcs to maintain defensible body-space.

Such sexuality as has survived the Sloane training goes into the sulky mouth (there is rarely enough to reach the edges of the lower lip).

Within the blast-radius the Sloane laugh can damage bone structure, and may cause a ripple effect in the cortical matter, similar to that suffered by professional boxers and high divers.

There is a danger of nervous rictus, of hyperoxygenation, and of swerving dangerously across two lanes of traffic when driving a laughing Sloane ('*Jesus* Christ, what was that?')

THE SMILE

The impenetrable smile remains one of the strongest of the Sloane defences and serves as a warning to the impertinent.

THE SLOANE VOCABULARY

Your thing – prick
Prick – old boyfriend
Old boyfriend – sexual encounter with a peer
Such a scrap – attractive
Fuck *me!* – old school friend has married a Viscount
Stiffy – formal invitation card
Can I stay the night, not to do anything, just to be close? – let's fuck (men)
Use your mouth – eat me
I'm not very good at that – oral sex makes me *sick*, I'm awfully sorry

Coming – Arriving (usually late, and for drinks)
Slags – Sloane girlfriends
Toilet – W.C.*
Rustic – sexually active
Somewhere awful – anus, or Essex

*From being the feared and suppressed word in the Sloane vocabulary, this is becoming more and more the norm amongst the upper classes. Aspiring Sloanes shudder when they hear it, and lose points by doing so.

NON-SLOANE VOCABULARY

Verucas

Shagging

DO SAY

Note: intricate defences of the class make penetration difficult, and ambitions should be modest. Researchers should be careful to restrict their social contribution to the following useful phrases.

When's the off? Wicca? Gerald Gin? Pass me that gentleman!
How amazing! That's where *my* brother went to school!

DON'T SAY

Money supply under control, think you?

THE SLOANE NORMS

The Sloane number of sexual partners by the time of the first marriage is twelve (she admits to five). She loses her virginity in Switzerland at the age of eighteen to someone she's only just met ('You don't want everyone *knowing*'). It is a tremendous anti-climax, but she says she enjoys it ('I'm glad to say I'm perfectly normal'). He offers to call her later in the week, but she refuses: 'Oh all right, but actually I'm frightfully busy this week.'

To her friends she compares the experience with a visit to her dentist and they all squeal (after History of art, squealing is the most obvious Sloane talent). The scrotums of passing men are tightened by the noise, fearing (and rightly) an animal caught in a trap.

At the Onanist dinner a non-Sloane man (note belt, shirt and make of shoes) reveals his origins. The Sloane man in the picture is asleep on the table.

Young ski instructor demonstrates the most favoured Sloane sexual position.

THE SLOANE SEXUAL PRESENCE

The Sloane in her pure form is a social, not a sensual animal. Linguistic sociologists have demonstrated in the 1982 analysis of questionnaires completed in street-surveys on a research axis between Gloucestershire and Park Walk SW3 that she is statistically 98 per cent more likely to choose the computer-modelled verbal unit '*Hi* how amazing, I haven't seen you for *yonks*!' rather than the modelled unit, '*Fuck* me! *Fuck* me! Oh my God, you're so *big*!'

It is important for prospective partners to realize that Sloane sexual intercourse is interpreted by the Sloane as a series of societal connections of which the end purpose is to expand her address book. This barter system allows her to reciprocate in kind for weekends in areas of high-stabling density without

The traditional coupling takes place behind the Queen (out of shot) and draws attention from Her Majesty. The purpose of sex is to increase societal relations.

becoming vulnerable to Capital Gains Tax. It has no cultural relationship with sexual connections formed by non-Sloane classes (except prostitutes, or philosophers who do nothing in bed but giggle).

However, anthropologists have recently identified the Sloane as having the largest single capacity for triggering sexual arousal amongst all major sub-Sloane genera, peaking with the owners of Asian mini-marts.

Characteristics listed in order of preference by a statistically neutral sample of sub-Sloane respondents revealed the following data.

On intimate contact with Sloane families, 68 per cent of Asian mini-mart owners say: 'The interest rates which the banks charge to us for our expansion are most regrettably 5 per cent over the interest rate charged to the fathers of the charming ladies, and we do feel that in consideration of the seeing-to of their daughters and the teaching of them, we should meet their fathers in the big banks of the City and arrange certain loans at the rate they charge their own cousins and this would be for the benefit of all concerned. Also to join their gentlemanly clubs, and to bid for the feet of the fox to be retailed from our freezer cabinets.'

Other comments included, 'In the words of a very old joke I want to do to them what they've been doing to the working class for two thousand years.'

Senior men: 'There is the occasional quiet weekend when one has nothing better to do . . .

Junior men: 'Awfully nice girls, triffic girls, rarely tremendously good value. I love the way

The senior man, cool, commanding, with rather small eyes.

The junior man, cheerful, pleasant, polite, and correspondingly less effective.

Sloane man attempts Rude Boy approach, often an effective alternative amongst an over-supply of merchant bankers – but only genuine Rude Boys can carry it off.

they *run*, with their arms all over the place, you know?'

Rude Boys: 'They're *gagging* for it!'

Poets: 'I want to grind her face in a bowl of liver, I want my lingual dyno-rod to explore her five blind orifices, I want to chew her face, take bites out of her back, I want to sluice into the depth of her as she wallows in a slop of emulsified offal, I want to bury my sorrows deep between her thighs.'*

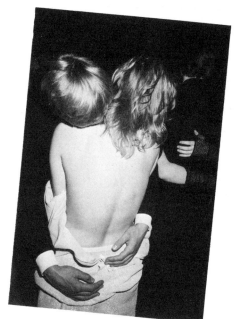

A perfect back inflames the poets.

It is notable that the level of sexual arousal had a high content of aggression, financial advantage, social insurgency and emulsified offal. These elements are only obliquely connected with sex in the well-adjusted psyche, and psychiatrists find it significant that the Sloane attitude to the world generates such reactions. *'Bit serious isn't he?'

PRELIMINARY SEXUAL STATISTICS

85 per cent of Sloanes responded positively to the computer-modelled unit 'I prefer a good laugh to meaningless sex', rising to 92 per cent for 'I think sex is tremendous fun but I can't understand what all the fuss is about'.

Other units attracting positive responses:

85 per cent: he is sweet, but he's a boy, just a boy.

83 per cent: I think a good bop is an excellent alternative to sex.

80 per cent: I think good silver is as important as sex.

79 per cent: I think Gloucestershire is much more important than sex.

94 per cent: I shall probably marry into the Brigade of Guards, for my sins.

89 per cent: Clarissa is a *slut*, frankly. She thinks that sort of behaviour is funny, but I don't think it's clever.

All Sloane men (by a statistical anomaly 104 per cent) respond positively to the unit:

104 per cent: I can't pretend to understand the mamselles, but you've got to get the dirty water off your chest now and again.

THE DIET

The bosom is prized as the Sloane's main offensive weapon and is developed early by disfiguring eating habits. But obesity is recog-

The Sloane bosom, often perfect for nine months between the ages of nineteen and twenty, promises trouble and pain at the age of forty.

nized as a lapse of taste, and a medical impediment to insemination. The result is strict regimes through the middle to late twenties. But owing to the class metabolism, when a Sloane puts on weight, the only way she can lose it is by sitting on a bacon slicer.

Light lunches, if at all (yoghurt, celery sticks, a glass of white wine). The diet preferred by models (eating freely, and throwing up in the Ladies' while the man pays the bill) is unacceptable to the Sloane sense of economy. For those on a calorie-counting diet, dinner is often a drinks party.

THE COMPLEXION

Facial complexion is the most highly prized feature of the Sloane. Generally it glows, radiant with youth and health, but this stops at the bra-line where nervous disorders (eczema particularly) generated by stress and social anxiety may take over.

The perfect Sloane complexion which men wish to hoover off the face with their lips.

Little make-up is used in the early years, but child-bearing and heavy drinking have a deleterious effect on the face, and the older Sloane applies make-up by falling face down on to her dressing table and working her features.

THE DRESS

Sloane libidos, like the feet of Imperial Chinese children have been constrained from an early age. The Sloane affinity for certain restrictive clothing (especially Scotch House breast-binding sweaters, riding trousers, ski-

The cheerful Sloane display indicates a lack of availability for sexual intercourse.

boots) is a psychic corollary of this, and display of these items purposely indicates an availability for sexual intercourse.* The double (but not the single) rope of pearls performs the same function, and for this reason is always worn when having dinner with a viscount.

*It should be noted that dresses cut low across the bosom, skirts split to the hip, holiday thongs and party nudity indicate precisely the opposite. The more that is physically revealed the less likely the Sloane is to allow you to plunge your face into her declivities as you hopefully kiss her goodnight ('Dooon't!'). The function of sexually arousing clothes is deliberately ironic and constitutes 80 per cent of the Sloane sense of humour (the other 20 per cent consists of being thrown fully clothed into swimming pools).

Underwear in these cases properly consists of knickers with an open gusset for convenient access when bending over a bicycle, vaulting from a mounting block, or when excited by Hogmanay (q.v., and Dr Kit Bryson's *Statistical Analysis of Sexual Apertures*, Harvard Research Press).

The hair is scraped back off the forehead with a Germanic severity and often held in place with a pre-teen Alice band. Psychiatrists are unable to say too much about this ('trick cyclists'). Although many Sloanes may dress like pirates, the pearls are a constant feature (see *Japanese Sloane Sexual Accessories*). Everything below the pearls may be interpreted as an ironic corollary of the pre-sexual doll's head above.

A sense of humour is dreadfully important.

RESTAURANT FOOD
(For Men)

It is important to set up a commanding lead by ordering for both of you, and – crucially, for this establishes the parameters of your class identity – to order the most disgusting thing on the menu. 'I'll have the brains, the offal, and the sorbet of sinus membranes to start, and Caroline, for you, the fox feet? Or the verucas? And I think the cold platter of sliced pig's penis, to follow, and what are the devilled haemorrhoids like today? We'll both have spotted dick to follow, won't we Caroline? Har har!'

CONVERSATION

It is reported (*Sociology of the Royal Palaces* by Dr Kit Bryson, Harvard Research Press) that the topics of conversation most often offered in a second-level social matrix (dinner party) at Kensington Palace are:

1 Prince Philip
2 Our erratic digestion (including explosive and unpredictable flatulence)
3 Episiotomies
4 Frequency of marital relations after second baby

These topics are formally offered (1. 'You'd think at his age . . .' 2. 'I find radishes are the worst . . .' 3. 'Got the doctor to put a couple of extra stitches in . . .' 4. 'Frankly I find Ovaltine more effective') and should not be taken as an indication of any interest in sexual matters other than an interest in talking about sexual matters as a technique of peer-bonding.

THE ELEMENTS OF SEXUAL ATTRACTION

It is statistically difficult to incorporate Sloane characteristics into an inventory of human sexual responses as Sloane triggers are only subliminally connected with sexual activity. However, the most powerful focus of arousal tabulates in the following way.

A virgin garden ready for planting arouses the Sloane libido more than virtually anything else.

Eton arouses the Sloane libido more than almost anything else.

Viscounts arouse the Sloane libido more than practically anything else.

SLOANE APHRODISIACS

Eton

Viscounts

Queen Anne Houses

Stabling

Trust money

Gloucestershire/Wiltshire borders

Hogmanay*

Bentleys

The figures break out as:

89 per cent – Courtesy Title.
80 per cent – Major Public School.
78 per cent – Taste in Shoes ('I *always* look at a man's shoes, they're more revealing than practically *anything*, honestly, *you* try it').
78 per cent – Stabling.
77 per cent – Sense of Humour ('What do you get if you sit on an igloo? *Polaroids*!')
75 per cent – Maternal Approval.
60 per cent – Sexual Ability (in terms of capacity to giggle in bed).
4 per cent – Sexual Ability (in terms of generating sexual feelings).

In a recent survey it was shown that 56 per cent of Sloane men were technically incompetent (as sexually impotent, or in terms of not knowing what to do with their hands) and that this was considered to be a positive asset amongst Sloane women.

*Hogmanay: this is the one night of the year when formal group relations are sanctioned immediately prior to the linking of arms and singing Auld Lang Syne. It takes the form of a sexual version of the eightsome reel. A rare photograph smuggled out of a high-security Dumfriesshire party shows the anthropological evidence for this traditional technique of peer bonding.

SLOANE TURN-OFFS

Anything boring

'Neurotic feminists'

Catering managers

Liberals

Jews

Rolls Royces

A sense of humour really is vitally important. Also to assume a pre-flagellational posture. And to show photographers what Sloanes really think of them.

PREPARATIONS

Swaine Adeney Brigg and Sons Ltd supply equipment which is adapted for use in the most important Sloane encounters – saddlery and tack form the basis of their only exuberant sexual activity. The hunting horn is used as an abbreviated enema appliance. The dressage whip (not pictured) is favoured by senior Sloanes, more than the crops shown, and the fox's head is displayed as an icon of sacrifice. The soap is used for washing afterwards (up to three days later).

Sloane sexual accessories. '*Such* a nice shop, it's a pleasure just walking in.'

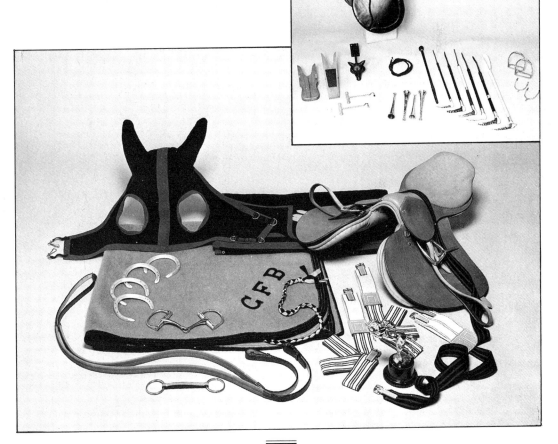

THINGS SLOANES ARE GOOD AT

Laughing

Squealing

Having lunch with their sisters

Talking about their boyfriends to their girlfriends

THINGS SLOANES ARE NOT GOOD AT

Grovelling on the carpet begging for sex

Wearing nothing but riding boots and black stockings, and bestriding Sloane men with a severe look on their faces

Wearing restrictive collars and eating reconstituted dolphin meat out of a dog bowl ('Oh *no*! Poor things!')

THE MANUAL ELEMENTS

How To Do It, Where To Do It, And Why

FIRST LOVE

The first affair, depending on fathers, capital base, and access to trust money will last up to two years and will be mainly spent in cocktail bars, on Honda 50s, in damp flats and other people's houses wondering how upset the other would be if they broke up. After bonding has taken place the sexual element is accommodated, but defused ('A sense of humour is terribly important').

The contact was made by letter direct from school ('I thought I'd pen you this epistle, I don't know why, I just like writing to you for some reason'). The affair suffers from a lack of physical movement during the act, on both sides (87 per cent reporting the major difficulty of not knowing where or when to put the hands).

CAROLINE, aged 28

'He's pretty amazing actually, really terrifically good looking, I *do* adore him, he's got such a sweet face, and he works at Peat's and always rings me up when I'm watching Crossroads to read me my Patric Walker and he's got this *awful* old Honda 50 which I *won't* ride with him on (he can't *drive* it!) and he calls me Porky when we're alone – he says it's part of a joke and it's *too* revolting to tell me what the punchline is – and I know he likes me because he calls me by my surname when we're at drinks, and sometimes at the Cod when I'm with some old schoolfriends he comes up to the table and says 'What are you slags talking about, I can guess!' and once he put a valentine for me in The Times on Valentine's Day! *Don't* you think he's precious? I *adore* him, and he really isn't greedy and foul like other boys, because when he went upstairs in Fulham to go to the loo he saw the sign on my door "No Men Allowed!" and he looked in and saw my five teddies on the pillow and he went downstairs and out of the front door and I *simply* can't get him on the telephone any more, what *do* you make of him, he's *such* a scrap!'

TANYA, aged 22

'We get on really well I suppose, we've been going out for two years, but he doesn't say anything when other people aren't there.'

SALLY, aged 20

'I don't think it's going anywhere. I'm afraid he's a weakling. He doesn't take me in hand no matter how badly I behave, I don't think he cares at all, in fact.'

BEETLE, aged 17

'We're getting married in June, the church is booked, Jenny and Caro are bridesmaids, Mummie's got the caterers and the marquee, Daddy's bought us a little car – I've written to the Colonel for married quarters – we're living on the base for the first eighteen months. I wish Rupert would hurry up and ask me, he's cutting it *awfully* fine, the invitations have to go out on Friday. *Typical!*'

INTRODUCTION TO THE AFFAIR

The Sloane seduction is spread over:

★ two evenings at the pub;
★ three lunches;
★ four dinners;
★ two full evenings on the sofa,

after which you may assume you are on a formal footing unless you get 'I don't think this is going anywhere', which may be mooted, between the anal phase and the flagellation, probably in Brinkleys, Hollywood Road.

For juniors the first act of sexual intercourse should take place after the first dinner – any longer than this without penetration makes it most unlikely the connection will ever take place. She will have made herself available once, as the schedule requires, and if the opportunity is not taken up she will never make herself available again. However affectionate she becomes you will be cast in a fraternal mode ('Such a pet').

Seniors will find their schedule more flexible, but rough trade and Rude Boys will find the schedule to be significantly quicker.

ROUGH TRADE

Independently wealthy Sloanes begin to declassify themselves (lack of ready money is central to the Sloane experience). The first sign is often manifested in a practice of picking up bouncers, butchers and black men outside Wormwood Scrubs with a rather imperious manner ('I'd like you to fuck me, will you?' They do, but reluctantly, '*Wot* a nerve,' their wives say.)

The act itself is a combination of boredom, bravura and alcohol and is used as raw material to be reprocessed into conversation. The impulse is not democratic but capricious, and it is difficult for yobs to position themselves for maximum impact probability. Nor is it always desirable, as the Sloane impulse is related to that of their male counterparts in wrecking a colleague's university rooms with vomit.

RUDE BOYS

More frequently and with the broadening of the category, it is becoming common for

Rude Boys may be in action out of shot making remarks. She may have just seen his white socks.

Sloanes to take an overnight holiday with an unsuitable stranger. Mrs Thatcher's England ('That *ghastly* woman') is commonly blamed for the dubious practice of hit-and-run Sloane sex ('And honestly, Tom, Jonty, Henry and Hudson just spent the whole night ignoring me, or calling me by my surname and I was *sick* of it!').

Socially unthreatening groups (Mancunians) are statistically over-represented in this area. They are also aided by an ability to give it 'a lot of that' (four flat fingers wag from the mouth). This represents verbal ability and generates squeals from Sloane women.

Though Sloanes are acutely alive to social threat they are unaware of sexual threat until it is too late. This is a matter of annoyance to many (87 per cent in a recent sample) London-based Sloane men. ('I mean bloody hell, Caroline, what were you thinking of, couldn't you *see* what he was like?')

To qualify as a Rude Boy candidate and be eligible for this form of social intercourse you should present yourself carefully. As in any bargaining situation your goals should be clearly defined. Your purpose is to disorient the target Sloane and reorganise her expectations ('Apparently they just do it all the time!'). Dress consists of a padded blouson jacket, rude-boy jeans and, most importantly, white socks ('He was wearing *white socks!* His jeans were too short and he was wearing *white socks!*') The most successful approach entails an easy assumption of authority (q.v.), saying 'All right doll, you're dancing with me now,' as this triggers a series of switches which floods her system with submissive enzymes. It is important to establish casual groinal contact within the first minutes, preferably via an expressionist dance style.

Do treat her approaches casually: *do* get her name wrong (Mandy for Candida, Sesame for Cecily), *do* tell her if she wore high heels her legs wouldn't look so fat.

Sloane: I love this record.
Rude Boy: It's crap.
Sloane: But it's Bruce Springsteen.
Rude Boy: It's crap. I like black music. Been to the Wag, have you?
Sloane: The where?
Rude Boy: The Wag club. Beat club. Best in London.
Sloane: I went to Tokyo Joe's once, but I don't normally dance: the last time I danced was at the Oxford Beagle Ball.
Rude Boy: The Wag's great. I've never been there without copping for it.
Sloane: Copping for what?
Rude boy: Totty. Copping for totty. *Skirt.*

Sloane: Do I count as skirt?
Rude Boy: If you like. If I undid that safety pin would your kilt drop off?

'Totty? Wall to wall totty, pal, gagging for it, they're sitting up and gagging for it. Look at this one, just look at her – you're one, girl, aren't you? Eh? You're one all right, come and have a dance, my word, you've got a pair of legs on you, you have, what do you do then? Y'*not?* Are you? You never are, you're pulling my leg! You're never a secretary! So am I, I'm a secretary myself! Do you know my sister Linda, she's a secretary too! We're all secretaries in my family!' (This continues indefinitely, and is a major factor in Sloane man's indignation.)

'Here, would you like to meet one of my boys? I can put him your way at fifty pee a dance, one pound a close encounter, and one seventy-five for tonguework.'

If preceded by a reputation for sudden and unpredictable violence you will find an automatic respect. The fact that she has no real interest in sex is an advantage to you, as is their desire to be amiable.

Note: copping for it once is always possible, but do not call her again. ('I hope you don't think I'm going to make a habit of this,' she will say.)

THE FORMAL INTRODUCTION

Note: Sloanes can say 'What do you do?' but a deprecatory *moue* is required. 'Boring question, I know,' has identified pseudo-Sloanes since February 1983.

DRINKS The question is, 'You know Jeremy, don't you, he's with Lloyds?' The Sloane response: 'If I meet another banker I'll *die!*' The counter responses:

The introduction may follow different forms, but at charity balls it should always be made before the wine comes to the table.

Junior: No, it's not banking it's the insurance division. Your father's a Name isn't he? I've seen him on one of our syndicates.
Senior: I haven't been a banker for five years.
Rude Boy: 'I'd rather be with the Woolwich!

CINEMA The question is, 'You know Caroline Cummin-Owen, don't you?' The responses are:

Junior: 'I've seen *Raiders* twelve times, hope this one's half as good!
Senior: (to introducer) I know Caroline Cummin-Smythe, do *you* know why she left Christies, they were rather shocked you know.
Rude Boy: Hi.

DINNER Sullen nods should be exchanged at drinks before, but nothing said until seated next to each other. Then:

Junior: God, isn't Henley awful these days, have you been recently? I don't blame you *one little bit!*'
Senior: I think your brother was one of my fags.
Rude Boy: (didn't turn up.)

A secondary version of the formal introduction (private function).

SLOANE PICK-UP THEATRES

Research has nominated these public drinking outlets as the nearest equivalent to American singles bars. Contact may be made by strangers if strict approach patterns are followed. Groups of available Sloane girls ('slags' in young Sloane-speak) gather at the indicated times in single sex groups, or with a protective Sloane man (often homosexual) as an honorary 'slag' Girls lean forwards on high stools presenting their sexual assets beyond the rim of the seat as a form of anal display. The agricultural background of the Sloane psyche leads to highly coloured conversation ('Frankly there's nothing wrong with healthy vulgarity') and they may cast glances at favoured men, saying:

'*Worgh!* I could really do him some damage!'
'*Wurgh!* Catch that one bending!'
'*Corgh!* Look at the apricots on that one!'

Your approach should be made with the words 'Is this a private orgy or can anyone join?' Sensing a sexual opportunity the hottest girls may turn away, affecting a sulky indifference. Tweak a nipple. Consult Sloane body language before taking decisive action.

Phoenix in Smith Street, SW3 (public bar Mondays 8.30–10.00). Take your Bentley and pay for drinks with fifties: these are the most mercenary set in the Sloane world, and will only offer themselves physically to men with the fattest wallets. You should make a point of mentioning your gross drawings from your company during the introduction.

Surprise in Christchurch Street SW3 (Mondays after 10.00). much patronized by aspirant Sloanes, many of whom are so inexperienced in the Sloane world as to demand anal sex before introducing you to their parents. Very pretty decor.

Anglesey Arms, in the continuation of Old Church Street, going north over the Fulham Road, whatever that street's called (Tuesday/ Wednesday Lounge Bar between 8.00 and 10.00). Otherwise unexceptional public house often used by Sloanes in first two phases of the Sloane Affair; in the absence of obviously non-Sloane elements the squealing after 9.30 attracts occasional raids by the R.S.P.C.A.

White Horse, Parson's Green (Wednesday/ Thursday, *inside*, even on hot evenings). 'It's a cattle market,' Sloanes say, and for this reason it has become commonplace (in 68 per cent of arrangements) to make a venereal inspection of prospective Sloanes on the premises, under the table.

Duke of Boots, in Chester Row (Fridays until 8, or until the M4 rush hour has cleared). Quickies may be obtained here, for petrol money, or from Sloanes anticipating an unusually boring weekend in Hampshire.

Note: The **Australian** has suffered a 12 per cent fall-off in Sloane patronage, and the **Admiral Cod** has suffered a 22 per cent pick-up in pseudo-Sloane trade. Both pubs report themselves pleased with the change.

THE BODY LANGUAGE

Anthropologists have demonstrated the non-verbal network of associated signals (NVNAS) recognized by the Sloane population to be as numerous and complex as those of gorillas or African wild dogs.

The signals are used to assert authority, demonstrate affection or appetite, to threaten, or to invite bonding, or bondage, or bamboo shoots (a delicacy appreciated by both Sloanes and gorillas though not by African wild dogs). As the Sloane female has a vocabulary the size of an intelligent dolphin this significantly

In this example of body language Sloanes perform a bonding ceremony (but note female Sloane's mouth is firmly shut and she is trying to absorb the symbol nasally).

extends the range and speed of communication.

As a highly complex system of cyphers, NVNAS also has the function of detecting and repelling strangers from the group. The misreading of any of these signals will result in a subtle but distinctive aroma being released which will cause the Sloane genus to turn slightly from the alien (an angle as little as seven degrees will be enough) causing them to disappear socially.

The origin of the signals is obscure in the history of the class, but anthropologists note a visual etymology with signals used in the field by medieval hunters, racing signals used by betting men, and early court etiquette where (from Henry II on) a sophisticated sign language (Court Hand) became a *lingua franca* throughout Eastern Europe.

Note: on recognition of any of these signals it is important to respond decisively. However, this cannot be a comprehensive glossary, and the author disclaims any responsibility for scenes resulting from a misinterpretation of signals.

PEARL SIGNALS

(*Fingering pearls on left*) You are attractive, but honestly, you are moving too fast. You really must let me get to know you better, then who knows?

(*Fingering pearls on right*) What a common little person you are. Do say something else so that I can laugh about it with my friends later.

SCARF SIGNALS

I am unavailable for sexual intercourse as I am at the height of my menstrual flow. (Note knot is fractionally above chin.)

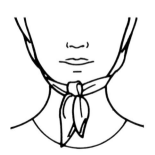

(*Fingering pearls at bottom*) I have an attractive pubic goatee.

GLASS SIGNALS

This subsection of associated signals is of particular use at high-decibel gatherings where verbal relations, being inaudible, are redundant. Commonly, both parties make unintelligible vocalizations, but communicate purely by body language – something which confuses and repels the outsider, as indeed it is intended to.

(*Thumb and three fingers*) I'm trying to keep a grip on myself because you're so attractive it's frightening.

(*Thumb and one finger on stem*) I do *not* propose to sleep with you no matter *how* much money you say you have.

(*Holding bowl of glass in palm*) I will squeeze your testicles at your point of crisis.

(*But with little finger cocked*) If your father is a Lord I will let you hurt me.

CIGARETTE SIGNALS

(*Thumb and two fingers on stem – neutral position*) Keep talking.

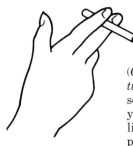

(*Cigarette in between two vertical fingers*) It's so easy to relax with you, we must know literally *all* the same people!

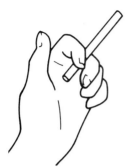

(*Cigarette between two bent fingers*) I am wearing no underwear. But don t get any ideas.

(*Cigarette between thumb and two fingers*) I haven't had a bit of rough for too long.

(*Cigarette in holder*) Sit up and beg, and it still won't do any good.

Sloanes of piercing their labia and securing their chastity with a primitive safety pin.

In the Sloane cultural gene-pool, the practice has survived in symbolic form, and the position of the safety pin (rising up from the hem towards the crutch) has significance in the following universally accepted terms for monitoring the progress of your courtship.

1   Your bearing is rather intriguing. But are you all you seem? I am cautious as I have been disappointed before.
2   Though you are sympathetic and I really enjoy talking to you, I do not yet find you attractive in *that* way. But these feelings may grow with time.
3   I am ready for sexual intercourse. But don't presume that this makes us intimates. It takes a lot more than sex to make friends of *me*.
4   My popularity is not due to my enormous intelligence. For God's sake take me back to your flat in Knightsbridge and give me the most frightful seeing-to. (Note safety pin on *right* of skirt. This signal is only used by rogue Sloanes, or Sloanes with a psychiatric history.)

VARIOUS SIGNALS

(*Hand under elbow and forearm hanging forward*) I am built abnormally large. Can you help?

PIN SIGNALS

Note: the significance of this ornament on skirts has a long social history and has been traced back to the practice of early Moslem

(*Four flat fingers held up to the cheek*) I would be interested to know how much money you had. Tell me. Whisper.

(*Elevated wrist, hand upturned*) Due to an annoying message from a clinic I am unavailable for sexual intercourse. But *do* try later, please, really.

(*Finger pointing left*) I am turning left.

(*Clutching at forearm*) I am an accredited expert in techniques of Oriental sex developed in Manila and perfected in SoHo. I can show you, if you'll come into the men's lavatory with me. I will not invoice you.

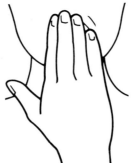

(*Flat fingers concealing yawn*) Your cleverness does not impress me.

(*With head up her dress, piggyback style*) You may think I find you attractive, but I merely find you amiable, and this is just as well as I am in a position to break your neck in a single spasm of my thighs.

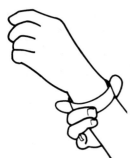

(*Twisting bracelet*) I have always been interested in bondage but have never dared to ask for it explicitly. Can you help?

FIRST PHASE ENCOUNTERS

Junior conversation should remain formal along the following topics:

Names: 'Nigella? Were your parents subconsciously after a boy? Don't want to get too Freudian!'
Spark plugs: 'My little Golf *simply* would not start!'

Jokes: 'What do you get if you sit on an igloo? *Polaroids!*'
Hangovers: 'I *literally* couldn't move on Monday, I mean Mondays are depressing enough, right?'
Palmistry: 'Here let me look at your hand. I'm actually psychic you know, I am, no rarely!'

Senior men address the same topics in these terms:

Names: 'Bentinck, as a matter of fact, James Bentinck.'
Spark plugs: 'My Bentley wouldn't start, but it took twenty minutes continuous activity to run the battery down. Engineering, you see.'
Jokes: 'I don't like jokes. Americans tell each other jokes.'
Hangovers: 'I haven't had a hangover since I was 12.'
Palmistry: 'Typist's fingers.'

Rude Boys say:
Names: Tel, Kev, Keef, Carrot Top and Razz (these are all criminal barristers and copy-writers making £28,000 a year).
Spark plugs: 'Polish my spark plugs anytime you like girl!'
Jokes: 'Your legs are too fat! Hahaha!'
Hangovers: 'No brain, no pain, hahaha!'
Palmistry: 'How'd you like to feel the back of my hand? Just joking darling, let's get some drugs and go dancing.'

Note: In the absence of immediate and casual contact – rare, but a form of brush-off ('it seemed easier than arguing') – do not expect to call her, but on meeting her again (you are now old friends) ask for her number and make obscene phone calls to her – she will enjoy healthy vulgarity. On meeting again you may ask her to lunch ('I'll probably see you at the Black and White Ball, but if I'm away in the country let me give you a call, we'll have lunch'. Or in Rude Boy: 'Been to the Gavroche? Come and pork out with us, it's on expenses!' If he does not wish to 'cop for her' that night, he will kiss her goodnight and then lick the

Sloane man and transvestite, 'It's important to be able to talk to practically anyone.'

underside of her nose as he jumps into his car. This reorganizes her expectations for the following time they meet.

SECOND-PHASE LUNCH THEATRES

Foxtrot Oscar, Hospital Road, SW3. Discussion of the name takes up the first course (a telecommunications acronym, 'Apparently it means f. off!'). The proprietor may not allow you to eat if he doesn't like you. You will be expected to put your head up her dress in the Bentley after lunch – this may be premature if Bentley post-1963.

Loose Box, Brompton Road. Many older Sloanes who have seen rough trade lunch here, drawn by the sympathetic name. Taking a younger Sloane here will be interpreted as a deliberately satirical gesture ('A sense of humour's terribly important').

Charco's, Anderson St. SW3. Basically sound, though some fluctuation in its reputation needs monitoring. Your friends know more about this than Egon Ronay. Rogue Sloanes wear no underwear.

Meridiana, Fulham Road, by Pond Place, SW3. Round the corner from Drakes which had a brief period of acceptability. The Meridiana has taken up the slack, and is *a bit smart*, but possible for Sloanes approaching thirty.

11, Park Walk, 11 Park Walk, SW3. In the key square mile for the younger Sloane. You may see Nicki Haslam passing.

Conversation for juniors includes:

Family: 'My great grandpa blew the lot – silly old fool – *but—*'
Schools: 'I was down for Eton of course, – *but—*
Counties: 'I don't actually live in Gloucestershire – *but—*
Hunting: 'I don't hunt actually hunt as such *–but—*
Jokes: 'There was this man in the park, okay? standing around with nothing much to do, probably out on his *lunch hour* or something okay? and he sees this *guy*. There's this *guy* who's digging all these holes, just beavering away digging all these *holes*, and the man stands there watching him for a while and after a bit notices this *second* guy, okay? following him a while later, filling in all the holes the first guy has just dug. And the man watches this and can't make head or tail of it, and eventually, to cut a long story short, he goes up to the first guy and says, "Look I'm probably pretty dim, but what's going on here?" And the first guy says, "No! That's not the second guy, that's the third guy! I dig the holes, the third guy plants the trees, and the third guy – no the *second* guy plants the trees and the third guy fills the holes in again but the second guy's off sick today!" '

or:

'Okay, I've got three jokes I'm going to tell you – there was an Englishman and Irishman and an Australian . . .

Senior men say:
Family: 'I believe they were mainly Governor Generals of Australia. Well, *someone* has to do it.'
Schools: 'Pop is such crap, actually.'
Counties: 'I don't think you'd get away with that in Dumfriesshire.'
Hunting: 'Stag are a pest where I live.'
Jokes: 'Governor Generals of Australia, as I say. Well *someone* has to do it!'

Rude boys say:

Family: 'Dad's in the Scrubs, Mum's on Supp, brother's on remand, and I'm doing credit policy for Citibank.'*
Schools: 'Manchester Grammar, A levels in Assault.'
Counties: London.
Hunting: '*Totty!* Get that totty's skirt over her head!'
Jokes: 'What would you say to a little fuck? And *you* say, "Hello, little fuck!" Harrgghhahahaha!'

*None of this is true, except Citibank.

THIRD-STAGE DINNER THEATRES

These are pre-sofa dates, prior to final decisive action (if this has not already occurred it may be already too late). Note: restaurants better than this denote a lack of ease.

Sambuca, 6, Symon Street, SW3. Prosecuting barristers bring girls here for final cross examination. Smart types start Saturday afternoon lunch at around 4.30.

Brinkleys, 47 Hollywood Road, SW10. Wailing Sloanes at lunch sound like the death aria of Rigoletto. This is where Sloanes come to say goodbye ('I don't think this is going anywhere').

Pollyannas, 2, Battersea Rise, SW11. The further from Sloane Square, the broader the accent. Sloanes armour themselves across the river with impenetrable vocalization. Ideal for girls to whom you have nothing to say.

La Nassa, 438 Kings Road, SW3. The Sloane haven of nasal sex, and a major contribution to

School Dinners where the food is the corporal punishment and the corporal punishment is nothing at all. The girl on the lap doesn't wriggle or squirm and if the man becomes tumescent the management will come down on him like the Metropolitan Police. The mixture is spooned into ears, nostrils, and hairline.

ARIES

There is a recklessness about you that finds favour in the Sloane sporting world – they like your bright eye, your athletic body, your off-the-bat manners. However, the spontaneous sexual connections which result from these qualities lead you into unsuitable company, with sales managers, out by the ring-road. Your impulsive nature was damaged in childhood and you need a great deal of reassurance but you are not clever enough to see this – you just think you have a very large number of friends (you haven't). You will not tolerate others saying how pig-headed the Ram is, and will offer physical and verbal violence to those who do. Your greatest Sloane asset is the certainty you are right in whatever you do, and the shameless way you switch sides when shown to be wrong. You are also helped by the fact you always have something to say – however trivial it is you find it interesting, and your mouth goes like a pair of castanets. But you are surprisingly insecure in your Sloane identity. You are the least controlled in the Sloane zodiac, and subject to the highest wastage rates. Perhaps for this reason you fear intimacy and when men get close to you, you punch them ('*Oh get up!*'). Party nudity is your greatest talent, and a weakness for exhibitionism makes you buy pre-weakened bras which burst at random under the pressure of your chest. When drunk you pull down your knickers and show your bottom out of a car window. This makes you popular with men, but when you bowl them over you become embarrassed. You are one of the few sexually aggressive signs of the Sloane zodiac (i.e. you have moved during intercourse, and once you moved your hips) and you are comparatively free of sexual inhibitions ('Aren't people *peculiar!*'). There is a wildness in you which you feel must be controlled (you are right), and you are susceptible to those of your social superiors with a weakness for flagellation, much as you protest. The senses of your being taken in hand causes you to relax and sigh with relief. But because it never lasts (you get bored not having your own way) a note of sourness and anger informs your increasing caution about men. Until middle age though, unscrupulous viscounts can spin you on your back and remove your underwear without even asking if they may. Your appetite for experience (which is what you call drinks parties) is enormous, and skilful men may use the momentum you build up to guide you into bed with little effort (being alone frightens you). But you often feel sullied by the experience (your language is frightful in disappointment). Even during the act you find yourself wondering what you're doing with this unsuitable thing ('You're *squashing* me!'). You can't bear to be thought of as a bad sport and freely consent to penetration outdoors, especially in haybarns (your sense of tradition is strong). But it is in your party mode that you excel right through your middle twenties (shouting, laughing, stealing traffic cones, intimidating waiters). Your most annoying characteristic is getting up in the middle of the act to change the record. Your greatest sexual asset is your forehand.

sinus problems amongst haute-bourgeois girls. Boxes of Kleenex are thoughtfully supplied by the management.

Golden Duck, Hollywood Road, SW10. Expensive, and Chinese, a contradiction in terms to the Sloane mind, but useful to reorganize the target's expectations.

Any Bistro Vino between Knightsbridge and the Earls' Court Road. Cheap, and you will be thought of as such, though many Sloanes have so little money it may be a plus.

Nineteen, 19, Mossop Street. Many Sloane Sluts here; and the atmosphere thick with garlic butter and sexual tension. Twosomes are keen for conversation with strangers.

Fingals. Sounds Irish, declassé. Very discreet, for illicit dinners.

Chelsea Wharf, Chelsea Wharf. Under new management; your coat will no longer disappear, and the serving staff no longer laugh at your order in high-coke giggles.

PRE-SOFA JUNIORS

Pre-sofa conversation for juniors* may include 'That's enough about me, tell me all about yourself'.

Her childhood: '*So* happy.'
Her boyfriends: '*So* sweet.
Her actual lack of confidence: '*So* surprising.'
Her digestion: '*Such* an enormous fart as I was getting into the *car*, right in his *face*!

*Juniors should remember: *don't* talk about previous sexual encounters yourself, *don't* scan room for new arrivals, *don't* say 'Toilet', *don't* live in Camden, *don't* attempt oral sex on first date, *don't* be overconfident (simply because you are truffling about inside her, don't make assumptions about your relationship), *don't* sit on her dog and break its back, *don't* be bisexual, *don't* be a dwarf.

SLOANE COUNTRY DIARY

The *nightmare* of moving in! Thank God we shan't ever have to do it again. Thank God we found a buyer for Harcourt Terrace, thank God we discovered Norfolk, thank God we found the Manor (though work needed *rather* daunting). Walked back from *pretty* church (had to thank God properly) past hedgerows blithe with May, and it's only April. Little yellow flowers with the tastefully arranged petals that people like, and the blue ones on their little stems that are attractive (darling). H. kissed me under a chestnut tree (*so* soppy) and made a most improper suggestion, but a car came by so he stopped (clot!). Saw pretty birds with forked tails, must find out their names, and the missile base.

Bottom (sore) up in the kitchen garden. Cuckoos and other birds, and a flight of Harriers (we're on the flight path – woe!) First blush of spring leading down to the perimeter fence (*severe* Yankee-dollar guards). Sunny meadows, huge five acres, with a wild wood and enormously overgrown bushes needing a shave. With H. feel nearer to God in a garden than anywhere else on earth (probably the brandy). Distant trees (*huge* ones – elms?) twinkle in the sun. Put in ten rows of lettuces with the help of P. Thrower Esq. Hedgerows thick with little violet flowers (violets?). In kitchen H. goosed the cook (me), but not in the kitchen, surely? No need to lock himself in study however – 'April weather, sun and rain together'. Have moles by the boundary hedge – 200-year-old hedge, but boundaries are Roman! Have acquired sweet cat (Bindy).

Jokes: 'Why do Japanese men have buck teeth and slant eyes? No I can't tell you it's *so* disgusting!'

Senior men do not let her talk about her childhood, her brother, her girlfriends, how she's not sure whether she's ever been properly in love, how she wishes she was eight years old again (see *Only Guaranteed Way Of Getting To Fuck Any Sloane At All*).

PRE-SOFA SENIORS

'You know, when I look up into the sky after a day's shooting and see the vastness of the natural world I wonder how there can be an afterlife.'

'I was always taught as a boy to be brave and kind, and that if I managed that I wouldn't go far wrong. I don't always succeed, I'm afraid.'

'You have a womanly look about you; I find it sympathetic. Girls rather bore me, I'm afraid.'

'A little viscount in the drive watching his parents pull away on the first day of his first term at prep school. I asked him why he thought it was that he'd been sent there. He said – and his glasses were *opaque* with emotion, but his voice was nearly steady, he said, "I think it's so that when my parents die, I'll be used to it."'

PRE-SOFA FOR RUDE BOYS

'Most girls like you have got no tits have they? they look like boys, don't they? because that's what their benders like, right? But you're different to that – I really like what you've got – *socking great dugongs* you can wade about in.'

'We found out the way he drove to work and we waited for him on the bridge and dropped a concrete brick through his windscreen, right? Then when his brothers came round that night, Nick, who's a criminal barrister, rings up two clients of his who owed him, and they came screaming round in a Jag, took these four blokes, one in each hand, and dragged their faces down the pebbledashing of my Mum's house. "Only too 'appy to oblige you Mr Briggs-Smith, sir, after what you done for Tel."'

HOW TO RECOGNIZE WHEN A SLOANE LIKES YOU ENOUGH TO LET YOU SEE HER NAKED

She will stare at you through unnaturally wide eyes (note: the Sloane man will ignore you altogether), rapid pupil dilation/contraction indicates inner contradictions valuable to your purpose. She will ask you where you live, how much money you have and where you went to school (lie if not major public school), and will tell you where her brother went to school (say, 'How amazing, that's where *my* brother went to school!'*) She will begin conversations with the words 'Now Henry, tell me ...' as though she is interviewing you (which indeed she is). Although miscegenation has been unusual (Sloane marries catering manager) it is becoming increasingly common as wastage rates increase ('Mixed marriages *say* unfair on the children'); but you will never be forgiven by the family for dragging her down to your own level.

When Rude Boys talk about sex acceptably at this stage, the Sloane will say, '*Oh!* You're revolting! No! *Pleease!* Stop mobbing me up!

*Except Rude Boys – 'Poor little bastard.'

The Sloane admires a strong hand, and protests are made only to inflame.

That's *say* foul! I wouldn't *dream* of it! I can't *believe* you would! She's *not* like that! They're *not*, they *aren't! Do* stop it! You're *so* disgusting! I can't bear it! I'm going to be *sick!* Yes I will be *sick!* And I *will* have another glass, *thank* you!'

ON THE SOFA: JUNIORS

You have sat up for hours waiting for her flatmates to go to bed. You join her on the sofa. She is sitting with her feet underneath her, smoking. She doesn't look at you. You have sat slightly too far away from her. Your voice remains casual, it is 1.30 a.m. and you both have to go to work tomorrow. She stands up to find another ashtray and sits without putting her feet under her (both pulse rates increase by 40 per cent). You work your hand round her shoulder. She relaxes imperceptibly. You say something and she does not reply. You either say, 'Oh here, I've been wanting to do this for ages' (73 per cent): or 'Sorry about this, I can't help it' (37 per cent), and wade towards her across the Chesterfield cushions sinking up to your wrists, and put your face close to hers. She angles her face fractionally towards yours and says 'Hello' (8 per cent – correct response begins with putting your tongue in her mouth): or, 'What are you doing?'* (78 per cent). Correct response begins by kissing the side of her face, working round in little kisses to her mouth. She does not part her lips, which are too firm to be welcoming, but you persevere, and eventually she does. After eighty seconds you pull away and say, 'Gosh I'm uncomfortable.'

'Actually you taste rather nice. It's that raspberry mousse.'

'You didn't mind?'

'No?'

'Do you mind if I—?'

'It's awfully late.'

'I know, I can't help it, I'll go soon.'

You should leave before she falls asleep. Put your hand just inside her Scotch House sweater, but it is an error to attempt to undo her bra (they don't undo).

Note: she will not come across this first night on this scenario. Sloanes who do not adhere to this scenario often have venereal disease – make sure you examine her with salted surgical glove for herpetic lesions before

*Alternatively, 'What are you *doing*?' (You have misread signals and should leave: 'Sorry, didn't realize you were *completely* frigid!'). The odd 16 per cent say nothing at all as they have gone to sleep.

Sloane man pushing Sloane girl's hand away from non-Sloane zones.

going into the bedroom ('A sense of humour is terribly important,' if she objects).

ON THE SOFA: SENIORS

The springs vibrate in sympathy with his voice and this causes a warm feeling in the Sloane lower parts. She does not know why.

'Don't say anything. Close your eyes. Turn over now. Lift your hips. Let's get you out of your jim-jams, you have been a naughty girl, haven't you?'

Remedial position for vertebrae sufferers. Orthopaedic equipment plays a significant role in early Sloane courtship.

ON THE SOFA: RUDE BOYS

'Here use my hanky, get that stuff off your face, this is a clean shirt.'

'What about the tart with the sulky mouth – think she'd like to come in on it too?'

ACTUALLY DOING IT

Or

'I Thought You Said We Weren't Going To Do Anything?'

SLOANES GO TO BED

Non-Sloane men make the mistake of getting undressed first and waiting under the duvet. The Sloane will poodle around looking for her fluffy slippers ('*Aren't* they hideous?'), letter from Mummy and a telephone number in Gloucestershire to give a friend tomorrow morning. A bright monologue fills the silences. She sets the alarm ('A quarter to seven') and jumps into bed so that the springs bounce. Reaching for her with a low groan will cause her to say 'Mm, nice and warm, you're better than a hot water bottle, I can't *bear* electric blankets, can you? But it's *so* freezing at home, Daddy's the meanest man in the world, do you want a cigarette? I'm *dying* for a fag, do you mind if I do?'

It is important not to be influenced by her cheerful manner. A barely detectable movement towards detumescence and she will quickly say, 'Oh dear – but never mind, it was lovely – *night!*'

Sloanes do not writhe ('Honestly, it takes *hours* to get the knots out of your hair afterwards').

SLOANES ABROAD

The major anomaly in the statistics occurs when Sloanes go abroad (not to Sloane colonies: Corfu, Verbier, the Dordogne or certain parts of Menorca where strict Sloane holiday romance schedules (q.v.) are observed) but to non-Sloane destinations (Trinidad, Lanzarotte, Galway, Budapest, Adelaide) where

Sloane in Lanzarotte takes advantage of anonymity to enjoy non-Sloane activities.

SLOANE COUNTRY DIARY

Horrid cat brought in *enormous* thrush, still struggling to breakfast table, where was H. when I need him most??? Both wings broken, self at a loss, had a medicinal brandy and used salad tongs to put the little chap in microwave – most humane thing. Poor little eyes melted and ran down his face in two big tears – *so* sad. Norfolk much as I adore it a bit boring at this time of year. Wonder how Pol and Lucy getting on at Christies, and Mummy in Sunningdale. Used to get into Bond Street in forty minutes d. to d. – not two and a quarter hours. Only visitors so far this month 1) the Vicar (old Face-ache) and the men to do the plumbing (had to pay them £200!) Tried to salt beastly bacon but had to throw it away in end and drive into Safeways (sixty-mile round trip). Saw a mole, and a negro in Norwich – didn't think there were negroes in Norfolk. Sad day when you don't learn anything.

Full House, and first weekend of rain and tempest – typical. Luckily all well used to cold (Eton has its uses). H. hadn't got enough beds in so Lucy on two-seater sofa, Tommy on two chairs, Miranda and Ed shared a camp bed and Johnny and Lucretia booked into the Country House for Friday night (they had to get back to the Smoke Sat. p.m. poor dears). But *such* helpful friends, the master bedroom is now habitable (have moved up the TV). but don't people write bread and butter letters any more? That frightful woman in Number Ten. Saw a *sweet* hedgehog coming out of border country beyond rose garden – H. picked it up and lobbed it fifty feet into copse – apparently he used to play cricket with them when young (*poor* hedgehogs). Took on staff, Mrs Wilson (looks like a frog).

TAURUS

The most naturally Sloane sign of the Zodiac – half the British Royal Family were born under this sign, as were all the World War I Generals and the early thirties Sloane hero, Adolf Hitler. An abnormal proportion of the modern Sloane world is born under Taurus, and the astrology most neatly describes the Sloane condition. You are slow, acquisitive, intensely status-conscious and rather stupid. Your sense of humour takes its raw material from physical suction noises and silly voices. This is dispiriting for your partners as they labour away on top of you ('*Neddy!*'). In your early years you may be so sure of what really matters that you live without sex at all, but your later years (if unmarried) will bring a sense of waste and disillusionment (especially as you put on weight) and you may embarrass your friends by chivvying men lighter than yourself towards the bedroom going 'Yum yum!' A sexually awakened Taurean is the most feared member of the Zodiac. Your natural caution combined with the hungry look in your face creates dangerously volatile situations, and confrontations result involving priapic men, cruel words and a long ache in the loins (particularly when you defend yourself with your feet). The countryside is your natural habitat, and your intellectual processes move at the speed of your crop rotation. You have a tremendous sensitivity to agricultural subsidies. This feeling for the land gives you a reputation for earthiness which is not always unjustified. Some few Taurean Sloanes do have a weakness for the flesh, and may eventually respond to purely sexual attention (though this will take several days of uninterrupted intercourse). However, you will be so demoralized by sexual fulfillment (it doesn't fit into your theory of society) that you will lie there like a big fish. It takes huge sexual heat for you to melt inside, and it is rarely men themselves who can achieve this, but their possessions, and wise Sloane men will goad you into a sexual crisis by repeating the insurance list of their household contents. You prize character more than personality, integrity more than talent, and dogs more than people. Your greatest love (a labrador called Tom) can never be consummated. You insist on love before sex as strongly as dinner before sex. It is love that redeems the act from its animal origins (something your farmyard mind is sensitive to 'What must we look like?'). You were formed by romantic pulp and familial lies, and consequently expected the act to resemble a psychedelic drug experience – entering a world of strange lights, floating bodies and no guilt. Without love you feel the reality is disappointingly agricultural. It is even more disappointing when love is actually there. Men do badly taking you to Chinese restaurants ('A whole table full of cat's heads!'). You are slow, but steady, and have a ponderous public speaking voice which (with the exception of Adolf Hitler) comforts and bores in equal measure (so reassuring in these troubled times).

anonymity and local whisky destabilize Sloane identity. In bars, in a bad part of town, Sloanes pen their knives, say 'serviette', dine with catering managers, allow negroes who have not met their parents to perform anal sex upon them ('I don't know *what* came over me! I *simply* didn't know where to put my head – and there were *plenty* of suggestions!').

SLOANE SEXUAL POSITIONS

The sexual position favoured by a significant majority of Sloane women was nominated as 'in a Georgian house near exit seventeen on the M4'.

FIRST UNION POSITION

On the first encounter it is common for shy examples of the Sloane world to curl into a foetal position round her bear, clasping her legs tightly and burying her face in her knees. The heels are left askew to provide for access into this sexual ovoid. You should not attempt to unwrap her (you may break something).

Other positions which research has identified as most popular:

During weekdays novelties are less common, and the Sloane hands are placed lightly on the man's shoulders, as at dance class. The back of the knees rarely lose contact with the sheets, except in case of cramp. The only variation commonly chosen is for the Sloane to lie on her front, in spite of the access difficulties (see *The Sloane Buttocks*) as it allows them to catch up with her Dick Francis ('There never seems to be enough time, much as I adore reading').

SLOANE COUNTRY DIARY

H. all over me like a hot rash (*sweet*, but makes it hard to watch TV). H. compromises by getting blue film – is *that* what it looks like! I suspected it looked quite silly but ça prend le biscuit. But I do adore my H. and in the words of the Master am 'ridiculously over-in-love'. Progress to house slow, still living in a builders yard. Plumbing kept us awake all Friday – H. in a rage asked the McKenzies (still on sofas and c. beds) whether they knew enough not to pull plugs at night. They'd gone before we got up (aren't people peculiar?). 'All I need is you,' says H., 'and a book of verse and flask of brandy' (*sweet*, I could eat him). Conker trees well out. Animals in the copse.

Sweet robins I can see on bedroom window sill this a.m., singing amongst thick apple blossom. H. tries to shoot at them with a steel catapult (brute!). Hunting fish makes him randy (my poor bottom). Letter from bank casts shadow over weekend – in their opinion I overpaid the plumbers so they've sent the cheque back (don't want to spoil local market). H. is explaining this with extravagant gestures and I walk into the back of his hand (stupid of me). What a shiner! Weather very hot and close, big swollen clouds sailing in from west. Garden enormously full, huge great standing plants (hollyhocks?) in kitchen garden, and tall grasses in meadows. Drinks before lunch and drinks after, or H. would have done the lawns. Saw a dead cat in the ha-ha. Not very funny. Wish it was Bindy.

A sense of humour is crucial.

toon characters indicating the hour). She will lie patiently and allow you to do as much as you like, but don't expect her to join in.

DOES A SLOANE TALK DURING SEX

During foreplay lively conversation is expected, based on mutual friends, and mutual jokes ('How frank Your Majesty is; if you hadn't said anything I would have thought it was the horse!'). However, during the penetrative, inseminating phase she prefers a demure silence (every Sloane values time by herself, and she feels never more alone than during sexual intercourse). When she does say anything it will be 'How are you getting on?', or more pointedly, 'Do you think you're going to be much longer?' Few other remarks are accepted as Sloane (see list). She may also answer the telephone.

WILL A SLOANE MOVE DURING SEX?

The only movement generally noticed is a slight elevation of the wrist (she wants to know what time it is). It is important for the Sloane girl to know how long it's been going on, and how soon it might be expected to be over (Cartier time for the luckier Sloane, Longines is possible but never a digital watch with an electronic alarm or jokey watches with car-

THINGS SLOANES DO SAY DURING SEX

'I can't breathe.'

'Oo! You've got a huge spot on your back – just here!'

'No! That tickles!'

'Ow! Don't do that!'

'*No!* I said, *don't* do that!'

The vital thing is a sense of humour.

THINGS SLOANES DON'T SAY

'Oh God, oh yes, oh please, please, please, oh that's beautiful, oh God I love it, I love you, I want you, don't stop, that's so good, give me, give me, give it to me, do it to me, you're so good to me, oh God I can't bear it, I want you so much, oh please, oh please!'

THINGS SLOANE MEN SAY DURING SEX

'Mm! I'm enjoying this part!'

'Are we getting anywhere down there!'

Your natural chirpiness helps you at parties full of strangers, and your ability to assume different and contradictory positions prevent you from boring yourself (others quickly tire of it however). You do not have too much personality but too many, one of which wears sheer stockings and a garter belt. Though your Sloane persona may be impressively detailed (you may even fall asleep during intercourse, so thorough are you), astrologers recognize it is often impossible to fault a schizophrenic's obsessive recreation of an alternative personality. You are the biggest frauds in the Sloane world, and the least secure – they never know what you are going to say next (any more than you know yourself), and this is hated in men more than systematic sexual infidelity in women. You bring long-standing affairs to an abrupt end by sleeping with a soccer team. You perform unnatural acts with eccentric men, and then walk away from them convulsed with disgust. Your emotional instability, your professional success, and your genuine sense of what is actually funny militate against any real acceptance in the Sloane world – you can't take things seriously, you're always laughing on Armistice Day and talking to tradesmen with apparent interest (it may not be real, but you do it too much to be healthy). You are often pretty, and sometimes attractive (though a bit clever). Your chattiness is useful in the early stages – you find contact easy to make, but Sloane men tire of too much talk ('There are only so many words'). However, men court you for longer than any other sign – you are a skilful flirt and can run three or four men simultaneously without being pressured into bed ('Darling, I'm *so* tired/drunk/stupid/bruised') as you recognize correctly that your elusiveness is your most attractive feature – certainly men find it so (particularly after they've been to bed with you). You can be promiscuous, as there are many points of entry into your private life. Though this helps your bulging address book (your greatest Sloane asset) it also publicizes your greatest Sloane liability: full sexual relations may stimulate a major shift into an alternative personality, or a past reincarnation, and it frightens your partner, especially when you get on top ('*Argh!* What are you *doing*?'). You are susceptible to other non-Sloane perversions – as a Mental Air sign you do not care to be imprisoned by the flesh and you seek release in images of other things. You are in fact the most perverted sign of the Zodiac, and may, for no reason you know, stand in a corner, provoke violence from yobs in pubs, pick up a motorcycle messenger in a lift and do it with him between floors. You may also practise cottaging, threesomes, voyeurism, transvesticism, and neurotic feminism, as rogue personalities break cover and take you away with them. you are so un-Sloane you may even ring up Anna Raeburn and The Doc to reveal your problems on the radio. This serious lack of reliability makes you the least Sloane sign, and you never lived down the story of when you were found standing in the corner, with a dunce's cap, naked but for your stockings, by your father.

NOISES SLOANES MAKE DURING SEX

Laughter is the most obvious auditory pheno-menon, and this is used to detoxify sexual feelings that may be inadvertently generated ('Sorry, I don't know why it popped into my little brain, but I suddenly remembered you trying to ride on Saturday, if *only* you could have seen yourself, honestly we were *rocking* with laughter, didn't you see us?').

She will also simulate a sexual crisis, if she thinks it necessary, though her partner may not notice – it sounds like a sneeze. Heavy breathing through an open mouth creates the wrong impression ('Do you want to try some of my Otrivine?').

NOISES SLOANES DON'T MAKE DURING SEX

Grrrr!

Argghhh!

Mmmmmmmmmmmm!

Ooblidah! Ooblidah! Ow! Ow! Ow!

THE TEDDY BEAR

However sexless the Sloane may be she often comes to bed in a man's shirt, knowing this may be unbearably exciting for Sloane men. It results in immediate emission (27 per cent) or impotence cause by overloaded sexual circuits (41 per cent), or a crying jag (12 per cent). All mark the end of the sexual encounter ('Never mind, it was lovely, *night!*').

SLOANE COUNTRY DIARY

I *can't* make Scotch eggs so there's an end to it. Just as well Gatlings cry off at last minute (stud in croup) and Tanya's housparty waylaid by Duke of Norfolk's fete. Take the hamper with H. up to Bickerdike's by our-selves, Constable country, heavenly. Picnic up in beech trees on warm day, dry leaf mould, so dark in the shade. Harvest going on in distance, priceless *Haywain* views. H. took catapult and nearly got a woodcock – me blackberrying by poppy field. Millions of Red Admirals round lilac tree in our sun trap. H. drinks everything we brought for party (pig) and snoozes. Thunderclouds build up but can't wake him. Sit in car for *hour* in pouring rain (so funny). Leave Bindy up at Bickerdike's and hope she'll find some other mugs!

Made rhubarb pie. H.'s whisky intake *pretty* impressive. Scoffed the lot and got awfully sick. Hardly surprising. When he went blue called the doc: how *do* you tell a relative stranger 'My husband is suffering from alcohol poisoning'? He seemed to think it was the pie (cheek!). According to Dr Know-It-All you aren't supposed to cook the leaves as well (waste not and no wanting I was always told). Honestly, these university men! Drove v. dis-gruntled H. to village hospital but (beastly cuts) had to go into Norwich (H. going absolutely *green*). Terribly thin wind today – 'Who doffs his coat on a winter's day will gladly put it on in May' (and June!). Saw a dead badger. Missed *Dynasty*.

The teddy bear is the Sloane's earliest and longest love, surviving into late forties.

As she slides under the duvet make no sudden movement towards her teddy bear (which she will defend, gripping it at a pressure of eleven pounds per square inch). You will have to talk to Teddy in a three-way conversation ('If Teddy doesn't like you, you'll be in trouble').

Three-way conversation with you, Sloane and Teddy Bear (be careful not to refer to lack of eye, ragged appearance or depleted stuffing – the Bear's life-history runs over the hour):

You: Well Mr Bear, what do you think of this? I think he likes me.
Sloane: No he doesn't, he thinks you're foul. Don't you Teddy?
Teddy: Yes.
You: Steady, steady, Mr Bear, you don't know me yet.
Sloane: He's seen your sort before.
You: Naughty Mummy.
Sloane: See Teddy, you were right, how foul he is. I'm awfully sorry, I don't think he likes you.
You: Can't have that, Mr Bear. What should I do to make him like me?
Sloane: *Talk* to him, *make* him like you.
You: How long for, talk to him?
Sloane: Until he likes you!
You: . . . I've got a little bear at home just like you, Teddy, it's a little girl-bear.
Sloane: Oh don't be horrid, Teddy's not interested in that sort of thing, are you Ted?
Teddy: No!
You: But where do little bears come from then, Teddy?
Sloane: Teddy's being sick, and don't call him Teddy, it's impertinent.
You: Teddy must be very proud having a mummy who's so like the Princess of Wales.
Sloane: (long pause) Night Teddy.

RUDE BOY'S BEAR CONVERSATION

'What's this fucking doll doing in here? Worgh look, he's had an accident, poor little bastard, he goes right round underneath . . . I got a confession, doll . . . I do too, you know, I had an accident too, feel, no, go on, *feel* – ha-ha, tricked yer!'

POOR BEAR

Rude Boys will dress the limbs of the doll in a prophylactic device and attempt to use it as a penetrative device. This is a mistake, and may cause a psychic haemorrhage.

A sense of humour is the most attractive
thing in a man.

H. not into work today. Told him he wouldn't
be popular with his boss. H. said *someone* had
to make sure the housework was done
(cheek!). Saw a whole group of rather dull-
looking birds huddled like a bunch of grapes
on a wall – probably lonely. Plague of frogs
which H. marches over in his green wellies:
Chief Frog Exterminator (poor little things).
Put them in the whizzer and try to cook them
('Eat your fill of that you kill' wise
countrymen say). Tasted so awful went to dinner at the Country House (£50 inc. bar bill –
outrageous! Struck off the service charge!).
But – unhappy day – H. has to blow into bag
on way home – it went a colour I'd never seen
before.

All day stripping down two kitchen chairs. H.
nagging what a tip the place looks, but he *will*
not hang my family portraits in dining room
so he's a fine one to talk. Grandma Hamilton
will do to hide a *rather* ominous patch of damp
by hatch till we can get men in. H. says we're
poor (isn't it awful, we have to save our pen-
nies). Explains it all over quite a lot of bran-
dies and I burnt the chops. The Country
House for dinner (£65 inc. bar bill – we can't
be *that* poor). Coffee at the Gresveney's, saw
the Jeffries too, and an animal squashed in
the road (*must* stop blubbing, H. says it's disgusting, makes face like a shopgirl's – he can
be really rather horrid).

CANCER

The pure sign of the self-created Sloane – the shell of the crab being the astrological equivalent of the navy skirt, the Scotch House sweater and the impenetrable pantyhose. Like crabs, too, Cancerian Sloanes smell better than they taste. Introspection worries you (for obvious reasons) – fearing the disorder inside your shell you live on the outside, and you are generally the best presented sign of the Zodiac – make-up, hair, vocabulary, manicure are immaculate. Much of your personal and sexual energies go into this prophylactic shell and prevents your real sexual nature from being expressed. But when your shell cracks and a man penetrates your interior there will be hell to pay. If he is inside when the shell heals he will never get out. You are the most easily hurt sign of the Zodiac, and can only be propitiated by an enormous dress allowance. The fact that you hide yourself encourages men to come after you, a sexual hide and seek. You may squeal during the chase, and men like this more than anything (certainly more than when they catch you, and you succumb to hysterical rabbit-panic, lying frozen in his hands). Your sentences begin with the word 'Mummy' more often than the word 'I', and this finally maddens men to be rough with you. However, your lack of internal knowledge makes decisions difficult for you. Because you don't know what you really feel your mind wanders during sex, considering the more straightforward aspects of your partner's abilities (i.e. his car, his prospects, and how much money he has). Being only peripherally involved in the act of congress you suffer from shyness ('Turn the light off, *please*') and hide under the blankets like a little rabbit, something which goads Sloane men into ferret-frenzy. You have a strong sense of intuition into the essential beastliness of men, and very definite ideas about what they should and shouldn't do, so you let them do very little ('*Don't* be awful, you're not really like that are you?') and you can run to fat. You insist on men talking to you after sex, something they're not equipped for, and your need for reassurance is greatest when their abilities are lowest. Trapped in your childhood the loneliness is sometimes unbearable. You have an unhealthy respect for love and fidelity – infidelity is theft. You were a virgin for too long, and prized your virginity so highly that your whole sexual being was polarized by the first encounter with a young French boy skiing one Easter ('I don't think this is a frightfully good idea, do you?'). You do have deep sexual resources but the sad fact is that the world is unable to exploit them. You need a tender but rather ruthless continental to play the magic springs inside you, and the sportive, cheerful foolishness of Sloane men is ill-equipped to do this – thus even though you are the epitome of the Sloane Zodiac you feel alienated. Your husband is too stupid to help, and you have a terrible, dreadful time when you're fifty, in an ashpit.

THE MECHANICS

When you first reach across under the duvet, then the Sloane body is cool, and often firm (especially if young), except for the breasts which generally have the texture of tensile plastic containing a high specific gravity fluid (commonly custard).

The bosom should be addressed with circular movements of a cupped hand in 3/4 time, extending the circle to her flanks. These may jump as you touch them (a subconscious effort to repel the hands). The Sloane learns this behaviour from fly-plagued horses, and she is unable to control it without deep analysis. You may also be tickling her. If she catches her breath do not assume it is pleasure or passion; it is (in 76 per cent of cases) an attempt not to laugh. Breathing into her ear will cause her neck to telescope 50 per cent into her chest ('*Tickerls!*') though she will encourage you to address the soft spots on her neck below her ears (if for nothing else than to keep your head out of the more embarrassing physical geography). If your head descends between her breasts and below she will lay hold of your ears, gripping them tightly at a point around her navel. A battle of wills can lock you in this position for up to a year.

During the penetrative phase the rogue Sloane may throw her hips sideways in a 9/8 bilateral rhythm (it appears random to the non-Sloane). This is not enthusiasm, but an attempt to get away from you, and often, in the case of men with short organs, successful. ('Stupid thing's fallen out,' is the junior response. 'Never mind, it was lovely, *night!*')

Working two sides at once is seen as unnecessarily technical ('Why are you doing that?') The weight should be taken on two pressure points – knees and forehead – leaving the body arched like a bow over the Sloane ('You look awfully uncomfortable.')

SLOANE COUNTRY DIARY

Midsummer church always makes me cry (H. furious). Vicar made rather dusty remark about attendance figures (not surprising with his awful new Series). Gardening like a mad thing, H. out shooting all weekend (never catches anything, I say probably after a completely different sort of game. H. gets excited and gives me a tremendous slap on the back, lose balance, catch eye on edge of table. Honestly, he's really *too* hail-fellow at times. Awful lot of moths around. Mrs B. in village had a fit and was taken away. *Little* anxious about the ba-bas. If H. insists on doing it his way we'll never have any family at all.

Melissa reports exciting Wimbledon final (she had my seat – me limping too much after treading on one of H.'s mole traps). H. expelled from Centre Court for shooting at pigeons in roof with steel catapult, what a scream. Sometimes wonder if he'll *ever* grow up.

Croquet party with the Thompsons from next village (she nice – but wearing a drab stuff frock, he *sales director*). Played into the twilight's, v. fat hunter's moon, bats flicking about conker trees and meadows visible down to the stream in moonlight. Old church bell tolled the hours. Think we all overdid the Pimms (H.'s mix) and *rather* a heated argument about the rules. H. swung mallet out on to lawn and caught Mr Thompson in ear. Dreadful scene after they left, I stormed out and walked into kitchen door – awful bruise down shoulder. I blame that jolly Pimms. H. Subdued this morning, and he's hung the paintings – hurrah!

THE LEGS

There is a spot at which Sloanes are vulnerable. It measures three-quarters of an inch in the softness in the crook of the knee, and it should be addressed orally. There are technical difficulties with the bedclothes: 'I have to have the blankets over me, it's cold/I'm embarrassed/I can't breathe'.

THE RHYTHM

Technical accomplishment is suspect in the Sloane mind, as is spontaneous and unexpected movement. The Sloane man may find moving to the phrasing of Bruce Springsteen's *Working On The Highway* a useful guide (especially the tricky bit at the end of verse 4).

The considerate man will not prolong the act beyond the limit of the song.

PREPARING FOR LIFT-OFF

The Sloane man will signal the approach of his crisis with a series of sharp breaths ('Are you all right? Do you want some water? Sorry, thought it was hiccups'), but he will go through the crisis itself without any physical indication it has happened (unsure of when to stop, whether to wait for her, perhaps she arrived first). 'Have you – er— ?' will produce the answer at any point during the act, 'Yes thanks, it was lovely, *night!*'

Portrait of the three-quarters of a square inch in the crook of the knee.

LIFT-OFF

The Sloane orgasm sounds like a yawn (very often it turns into a yawn) and is accompanied by slight pressure from finger pads around the hairline.

WHAT SLOANES THINK ABOUT DURING SEX

That the genus says nothing during intercourse should not be taken as evidence that nothing is going on in their head. Sloanes are unavailable for sexual communion as they spend the time exploring the memory of hot bodies dressed for tennis and two hot faces sticky with lemonade, in some haybarn, years ago, before the bypass went through.

POST-COITAL CONVERSATION

'Oh dear Teddy, don't look so disapproving.'

'Who are you taking to the Black and White?'

'Sushi says Jeremy makes her practically stand on her *head*, isn't it awful? She has *such* fine hair, and it gets all knotted up at the back of her head, it takes *forty minutes* to brush it out in the morning, don't you think that's foul?'

'Do you mind if I brush my hair?'

'What's the answer? Do you know what the answer is?'*

There may also be a further examination of your social assets to determine suitability for subsequent encounters.

*Rude boy says, 'Twenty-four'.

FARTING IN BED

Three reactions have been statistically analysed (*Intestinal Gas In The Dormile Facility*, Dr Kit Bryson, Harvard Research Press).

Juniors: ignoring it and breathing from top of lungs.

Seniors: clamping sheets under chin ('God, sorry, I wouldn't go under there for a moment if I were you').

Rude Boy: flapping sheets above head, going, 'Phwarrgghh! *Christ!* Oh dear!'

Note: Sloane men feel more about World War I than they do about their sexual partners, and Armistice Day produces similar symptoms (constricted chest, irregular breathing, swollen throat, open tear ducts). Sloane women generate the same symptoms in front of a lifeless Dutch Elm, or a campaign ad for baby Harp seals.

It is important to differentiate between these symptoms unless you happen to be a) a military historian, b) a dead seal, c) a dead tree.

BE CAREFUL

However sentimental you feel do not kiss the sleeping Sloane. If she wakes suddenly she may take off the tip of your nose in her teeth ('You *startled* me!').

Do not attempt to answer any of these questions:

'What *must* we look like!'

'Do you really think she was virgin when she married?'

'What will you tell your friends about this?'

SLOANE KISSES

Most often these are small and dry, or so wide open that nothing inside is detectable. The most feared of the Sloane kisses is when she pushes her tongue into your mouth like an

The perfect Sloane kiss, yearning, but never quite reaching.

erect wedge of beef and leaves it there. She moves it by rocking her shoulders. Only by this way can she communicate to a Sloane man her distaste for actively engaging in oral sex. Girls with voluptuous lips may protrude them, to expose the soft insides (it looks like an octupus turned inside out).

THE ACTIVE SLOANE

The engagement and the early honeymoon are the only glutting seasons for Sloane sexual intercourse (sportive Sloanes are game for anything – in the first stage parents expect it, and in the second there is nothing else to do). The man is surrounded by magic (the promise of a Queen Anne house before they're forty) and the woman spreads herself as she only knows how, like a cold collation. The magic may work on her insides with the force of a microwave ('We're going to be *so* happy!'). Love gives her the courage to go a few steps into his shadows. But as the light fails, she becomes aware of an unfamiliar landscape, and dark water moving, and there are shapes sailing under the surface, and a dead dog, possibly Tom, floating in the tide. This is why a sense of humour is so important, and what Teddy thinks.

STAG NIGHTS

Junior celebrations in pay-as-you-eat restaurants are among the dullest in the Sloane social world, and wilder elements slip out for a pint between courses.

Senior stag nights incorporate traditional features of prenuptial celebrations, including a fist fight, a food fight, and prostitutes circulating under the table attending to ageing and inebriated guests. The groom is expected to effect a form of coitus among the cheseboards. Juniors are suprised to see the sexual organs of their social superiors, especially when they are fifty, married, and live in Queen Anne houses off the M4, and most especially when the organs are grey ('Gypsy coloured, actually, not a pretty sight').

THE MOST FERTILE FUNCTIONS

No Sloane will sleep with you after a dinner party (her friends will all know), but they may do so after a drinks party, or a ball ('I wanted the night to go on forever. Not that it did'). The last night of a country weekend is profitable, but no unattached Sloane will be the first to do it ('I much prefer to keep a flirtation with a friend who's rarely good fun, than something heavy and not see them again – do you know what I mean?').

Sloanes just want to have fun ('You know it rarely *has* been good when you can look at each other the next day and *still* be giggling'). Though they dislike shocks they love surprises – and revealing parts of their bodies (especially *their* bodies) can be the only surprising thing about them. The men display

SLOANE COUNTRY DIARY

Mrs Wilson *has* to go (pilfering). Told her she *had* to go and she refused! At least she could make the beds then, but she's busy in the dining room polishing bottles (polishing them off more like) So hard to get help in the country H. says, probably right. Saw a bird sitting on its nest, sweet. Went down to stream to get rushes – saw a man fishing. Ranelagh's for the weekend. Woke up this morning feeling I'd been in a fight – *such* a sore tum. H.'s hand bruised, poor dear. Mrs Wilson left Saturday after dinner covering half her face – too ashamed to look us in the eye – H. did the honours, I'm proud of him and showed him so. V. sore bottom. Ranelaghs gone before we'd got up – aren't people *peculiar*!

H. has had a long summer holiday this year. Hope things are well with him in the City. Get a letter from the bank three times a week and they say we can't have stabling this year, or central heating, or do the first floor – *so* mean. Batten down the hatches for a v. squalid winter. H. working on a prospectus in his study for a private deal – brandy helps him think, he says, when he says anything.

Village fete in aid of mental defectives. Embarrassing trying to tell which is which. Mine only stall which sold *nothing* (loonies!) so H. is in for a big treat when he comes up again next week. Staying in Melissa's flat in town, and comes up nearly every Friday afternoon, or Sat. a.m. when he's too busy. All that travelling, poor H. Are people dull, actually, in Norfolk? Quite diff. from Lon. (*such* fat ankles, and the teeth! Fete next year for dental defectives!!!).

69

What would we do if we didn't have a sense of humour?

their personality. The momentum built up may be sufficient to divert the Sloane into bed. But ease, assurance, confidence and speed over thin ice is vital. Dawn has a morbid effect on the Sloane sexual vulnerability. She feels her spirits going out with the tide of night, and the glamour of the evening becomes a dream, burned off by the sunrise ('Oh you put that *beautifully*, I'm *so* glad you understand' – a decisive step into the fraternal mode, and disastrous).

THE SMILE

Drawing back the lips and baring the teeth is, in chimpanzees, a sign of aggression and fear ('Those ghastly teabag ads!') but may indicate something else in Sloanes, though anthropologists are still unable to say quite what.

THE ONLY GUARANTEED WAY OF GETTING TO FUCK ABSOLUTELY ANY SLOANE AT ALL

A Sloane in her pure form, like her dog, is trained to respond to the voice of command, and she prefers to be sexually subdued by being barked at. Even strong-willed, sensible Sloanes who stand no nonsense prefer this military technique of seduction. Make her respect you at once by barking. Show her you like her by ignoring her in public. Call her by her surname. Drag her out of parties. Take her to the Gasworks restaurant to meet criminals. Order her dinner for her (q.v.), laugh at her

their feminine side, or they display themselves (or in the case of Dai Llewellyn, both).

Exposed thus they feel the glamour of their peers' approval while revealing something of

LEO

Many dislike you but it is your talent not to notice. It is rare in the Sloane world to be criticized for being too noisy, too stupid, too overbearing ('*Be* a pet for me, oh *do!*'), and you cannot understand criticism when it is made ('Stick it in your ear!' you say in your haute-bourgeois, street-fighter's way). But there is a lot of you (as you say about wine you bring to dinner party, 'It's not very nice but there's an awful lot of it!'). So eager for admiration and social success that in your early days you were indiscriminate, and eligible men, properly spoken, could pick you up at drinks and be done with you in six hours (a Greek dinner and a compressed schedule on the sofa). For three years they jumped and pumped and you allowed yourself to be jumped on and pumped at. Few called you again and your social life began to slow – only for this reason did you begin to increase demand by decreasing supply. The lack of admiration caused you to wither, and now you are more susceptible to anorexias and frigidity than any other sign. The early reputation encourages men to act boldly with you, and indeed your extravagant language leads men to believe you are fond of them. All too often you aren't even fond of yourself, and getting you into bed needs limitless applications of money, flowers, and personal compliments, though courtesy titles can quickly reduce you to a state of pathetic acquiescence. Your need for admiration is a hole in your armour through which a large number of men come piling through to make pigs of themselves, sometimes more than one at a time – it is a genuinely social occasion. One man is not enough, and you see yourself in your deepest secrets surrounded by naked marquesses, in a trench of flesh, wallowing, that is, in their admiration, as if in a hot mudbath. You tend not to join in yourself, fearing to expose yourself to ridicule. This fearlessness surprises stupid men, and their disappointment leads to resentment. You have a neurotic need to be the centre of attention, and are one of the best flirts in the Zodiac: you perform confidently at lunch and early drinks. Dinner à deux finds you increasingly brittle as the goodnight-grope approaches. This is why you are so chilling on the doorstep, with your bright eyes and pained face; '*Such* a nice evening, you *will* ask me again, *promise* me you'll ask again?' The flirtation goes astray in bed though where you languish with your teddies, as if on some sofa surrounded by admirers. Your partner feels rather left out. You are a soloist, not an ensemble player. You place yourself firmly in the middle of the drama and play up to the audience. It drains you, and you take off your make-up afterwards in a state of complete isolation which only much later (when you're fifty) strikes you as rather sad. Your personal charm, like your hairstyle, conceals your lack of genuine bone structure, but how glad you are of it – so many have neither hair or charm, and it is just as well the fringe Sloane world prefers the charming to the good.

little secrets, remember she despises weakness, get into a fight with someone smaller and win it, using violence. Charge the net and fire volleys at her feet. Pay with a Coutt's cheque and no cheque card. Give her your collars to iron. Smile distantly and suddenly become bored with her; laugh loudly with friends who have stabling; look at her with a brief interest and let this alternate with a sort of blank stare; suggest improvements to her hair ('Cut it all off, *all* of it'), draw oblique attention to her weight problem. Invite her without warning to the country. Drench her with a walk in the rain. Dress her in your mother's clothes. Overwhelm her with a fourteenth-century bed. Leave her bewildered after dinner, and then come to her at 3 a.m., saying, '*Don't make a sound – the dogs are out!*' Then fuck her.

SLOANE SEXUAL ACCESSORIES

At your point of climax a Japanese Sloane will jerk her pearls from your anus to simulate a combination of orgasm and diarrhoea. This excites at least one basic interest of the Sloane world ('digestive irregularities' was nominated by 58 per cent of all Sloanes as the dominant topic of after-dinner conversation). Chicken vindaloo is a popular aphrodisiac for the same reason, as are enemas. This is linked psychologically to the anal relationship existing between Sloanes and their male counterparts, and between Sloane men and their housemasters.

Note: no Sloane will own a conventional

vibrator (unless to amuse her circle at Christmas), though she may often be seen in Sloane Street with her skirt round her waist, perching on the vertical fender of a roughly tuned Bentley ('That's better,' she says, she does not know why). The lack of this chrome feature on modern vehicles is why Sloanes disparage post-1963 models, in spite of the superior acceleration, handling and stabilizer bars.

RENAULT TURBOS

To confine the sexual arousal of Sloanes by the right sort of owner, Renault now restrict sales to applicants who have been proposed and seconded by two existing owners, and this application may be blackballed in the monthly ballot of all scheduled Renault Turbo owners. If you as a Renault Turbo owner have not been consulted recently you may wish to challenge your rating with Renault's London office, in the event of your having been struck from the schedule by prejudicial reports on your social credit.

Note: no Sloane has had sex in a car that weighs less than a ton.

SLOANE COUNTRY DIARY

H. punched me in the face! *What* a surprise! I fell over I was so surprised! He didn't mean to, needless to say, my fault for moving, but my stupid nose has gone. Bruise goes well with my eye (the one that caught the table). Saw a young dog fox (what's the fem. of dog fox? Cat fox?) disappearing into bracken. Rang local hunt but nothing they can do apparently. Dreadful man Scargill at it again. We have *mice* which Bindy (she's *back*) is too lazy to catch, but the beastly creature brought in a hedgehog by the throat and killed it on the kitchen floor – ugh! 1,400 brace of pheasant shot on Lord Normanton's drive. H.'s total: 2. It was when I laughed that he swung his fist at me, playfully of course, my fault for moving.

It's happened at last, I'm in pig. *So* wanted to tell H. but he was v. late in (working much too hard) and he fell asleep at once on the sofa. I shall call her Sophie. H. burst into tears when I told him – went to comfort the sossidge and accidentally caught my cheekbone on his elbow (*what* sharp elbows!) He tried to comfort *me*, and I bashed my nose on his forehead and the stupid thing broke again! Lack-a-day! All the swallows on the phone wires joining up for a chat before migrating ('Where shall we go this year?'). Masses of Michaelmas daisies and butterflies. I'm so happy.

SLOANE SEXUAL ECCENTRICITY

THE ACADEMICS SAY*

Computer research on local government employee files has shown that individuals who work in uniform are statistically more likely to abuse children sexually than those who work in deregularized clothing. Correspondingly, the Sloane phenomenon – uniform-based in terms of dress, presentation and behaviour – suggests an unusually high susceptibility to sexual aberration.

Happily, data does indeed show that primary fixations rooted in pre-sexual experiences organize Sloane sexual nature into an uniquely inflexible grid.

It is for this reason that psycho-anthropologists have investigated the Sloane genus, recognising in it the most fertile class for sexual deviation available for research and experiment.

*'They can say what they like as far as I'm concerned, I can't understand a word of it! Luckily I failed Mods and was in the City before I was 19, best day's work I ever did!'

THE FORMATION OF THE SLOANE SEXUAL IDENTITY

Analysts working on the mechanism of sexual deviations have isolated the influence, greater even than 'Mummy', 'Daddy', or the 1,000 lb vibrator called Poppy on which Caroline trots through puberty. The key organising principle on a total of 47 per cent of all Sloanes nationwide has been shown to be the death of their first dog (a Labrador called Tom). This gives a morbid cast to the Sloane in her sexual mode (particularly to her post-coital conversation 'Do you ever wonder what it's all for? I'm all right really, just being silly'). The morbid element is reinforced by parental discipline and the caning of their brothers at country public schools.

As the relationship between domestic servants ('Mrs Wilson-Without-Whom-We-Couldn't-Do') and the domestic establishment has been categorized as psychologically anal, a powerful matrix of interconnecting values, instincts and environmental pressures works on the Sloane mind from an early age. This leads to the theory of Submissive Dominance, and informs 86 per cent of all Sloane sexual relations.

THE THEORY OF SUBMISSIVE DOMINANCE

Psychological scientists interpret the submissive posture which Sloanes eagerly adopt in the presence of authority (policemen, any MFH, a Coutt's chequebook) as a morbid appetite for discipline, and have extended this into a general theory suggesting that all Sloane sexual arousal will be informed to some degree by sado-masochism.

Practical research indeed confirms this. A wide-ranging analysis of data (Dr Kit Bryson's research paper *Authority and Excitement*, Harvard Research Press) goes a long way to substantiate the thesis (the analysis of itemized call-girl invoices from the Home Office computer are particularly telling in the matter of Sloane men). The female evidence, scientifically based on EEG findings, pupil dilation, salivation, and a slight shaking of the fingers demonstrate that Sloane women are unhealthily interested in corporal punishment.

The appeal of and reverence to service dis-

VIRGO

'It's not *fair* we get *such* a hard time from astrologers, and we're not *that* bad,' you say, with an attractive sense of resentment. But, of course, you are that bad, and your only experience of happiness is relief. You are careful not to take the lead in anything (too lonely out in front) and you find greatest comfort in a crowd, with the women wearing hats and gloves. The blinding personal contact which sex promised you has been very disappointing. Damaged from an early age by clumsy subalterns you take a dim view of any enthusiasm, but sexual enthusiasm you find deeply suspicious ('What's he after?'). The purpose of sex is marriage, and the purpose of sex after you are married is to get a separate bedroom. You feel men will betray you (you were betrayed once, so you know), and friendship is far more reliable than love. Continental men make you nervous ('Oh dear!') but you thrill to the timbre of officer accents, and do well as Sloane vice-captains. Organized from an early age you become able followers, great disciplinarians. This cannot be regarded as a sexual deviation as it has so little to do with sex, but it is your most effective mode of entry into intimacy. Experience teaches you to despair of love, and the act itself you find vaguely unpleasant and embarrassing, like sharing someone else's bath-water. But you embrace pain inflicted by disciplinarian boyfriends. It hurts, but that's how you know it's real. You are sturdy under the rod. You perform reluctantly under sexual conditions but your sense of submission is socially attractive. You lie uncomplainingly under senior men, face down in a pillow reciting the kings and queens of England (Willy, Harry, Richard One . . .). However your sense of authority over those beneath you is a major factor in your resented reputation – you can't bear weakness, or men sobbing. Moral laxity (losing a job, remortgaging your Queen Anne house, sleeping with a man who has no money, marrying a sales director and living by the ring-road) makes you physically sick. When young your accommodation may look like a rubbish tip, but when you finally move into the flat in Harcourt Terrace, or the Queen Anne house in Gloucestershire, it is as clean as an operating theatre – something that suits your attitude to sex. Anaesthetics and implements of incision are common with Sloane Virgos, and this is why satisfactory sexual relations have the shock of major surgery, keeping you very much to yourself in subsequent weeks. You have the greatest sexual resistance of any in the Zodiac, though men sense your deep submissiveness, and are keen to take you in hand and treat you badly. But you can nevertheless hold out for years against bribes, pleas and promises – if they knew what they were doing you feel, they would simply take you without asking. But you are skilled at having men pay for you, and often your rent comes from a source other than your pay cheque. You give nothing away, certainly not yourself, but at least men don't have to suffer confessions and your little secrets. They do have to suffer your outstanding sense of superiority however, as they let themselves down on top of you. If only you weren't so declarative about your attitude to sex – the congregation at your wedding is embarrassed by the sound of your knees locking together as you walk back down the aisle. You have a very un-Sloane respect for education (getting *on* isn't really the point is it?) but you redeem yourself with a scathing disrespect for 'eggheads'. Nonetheless, alone in the Zodiac, you pass your accountancy finals first time, and this can be a moment of greatest sexual vulnerability. You know that men are only after one thing, but what that one thing is you can't find out.

cipline, the exaggerated respect for authority, the composition of the Sloane buttock (q.v. page 37), and the impossible behaviour of boisterous Sloanes in public houses are designed and developed to stimulate an atmosphere where corporal punishment becomes a natural corrective towards conventional Sloane behaviour.

Only in this mode of submission and surrender does the Sloane girl experience the full flowering of her personality, interconnecting all significant psychic experience. Not only through the Sloane life but through Sloane history as well. In this mode the Sloane finds herself in the presence of her father, her schoolmaster, the village bobby on his bicycle, the Brigade of Guards, the Duke of Edinburgh and Henry VII. It hasn't got much to do with sex, but it has a great deal to do with society, and as the purpose of sex is to increase her social contacts the pain is a small price to pay.

Administrators should note that Sloane women may object in the early stages to the administration of corporal punishment (particularly if you have only just been introduced). There will in many cases be preliminary resistance (37 per cent statistically acknowledge a reaction of surprise varying from 'I was quite surprised' to 'I was astonished, frankly').

Research appears to show that it is important to persevere in the face of her protests; to abort the project before severe pain has been inflicted will result in marked loss of respect ('You're *sick*! You know that don't you, you're *rarely sick!*') and restraint may be necessary. The practitioner commonly prepares a slip-knot in her Pony Club tie before making his intentions explicit. He then catches her wrists by a simple stratagem, and lashes her to the bedpost; experience shows the feet need not be secured as the Sloane finds writhing-room desirable. Soundproofing of the house may be necessary.

There may be unexpected consequences ('My turn now'), but be careful not to let familiarity breed a loss of dignity. The smack of firm government is her aphrodisiac, sexual equality being a symptom of 'neurotic feminism'. For this reason you should introduce the regime early in the relationship – most commonly between the first and second lunch date, somewhere between Brinkley's and 11 Park Walk.

The girls with the strongest appetite for this form of social intercourse may be found in pubs leaning forward on their tables, pushing their buttocks out from their stools in cotton stretch pants, often striped. The sociology expressed in this practice constitutes a concise expression of Sloane beliefs about the world, including relations between the classes, the sexes, the rise of trade union power, and the necessity for Cruise deployment. It is her primary, indeed only, contribution to political debate.

Note: she may need time to collect herself, but don't leave her tied to the dormile unit for more than four days.

INTRA-COLONIC INTERCOURSE

This form of intercourse is the succinct form of the submissive posture in which the genus finds itself most comfortable: 'I wanted to give him something special' (5 per cent); 'It keeps me in my place' (65 per cent). A variety of interconnecting social and emotional matrices combine with old taboos to give it potency. Before she will persuade you to perform upon her she will introduce you to her parents. And indeed this introduction ('Sir. How do you do') may be taken in 87 per cent of cases as a request for this form of domination. Her simulated resistance is an important element in the formal progression (particularly if you haven't

LIBRA

Though you enjoy arguments you hate fights, and consequently find yourself more often than you'd like in strange beds – clever men use your sense of natural justice to make you pay them back for dinner. But you look at the ceiling concentrating on the arabesques in your head, and the history of art (you got a C at A level). Your sense of beauty, harmony, and a good profile make you an easy pick-up in the showroom at Christie's or Sotheby's ('Oh *wasn't* Arnolfini clever? Don't you think?') Your over-developed buttocks flash signals at Sloane men, and this makes you obvious in a crowd – something that embarrasses but not wholly displeases you. You wander casually about wearing a rather attractive ensemble and a cool little smile. There is a promising lilt in your hips, and your skirt swings as you move. You appear to know better than everyone else, and this draws men to you who are keen to show you otherwise. Sloane men find you rather too clever ('All this arty business'), and somewhat remote. You want something magical and difficult, incredible intimacy tinged with a sense of danger, purity touched with perversion, a seat at the best table at the Black and White, with everyone laughing at your jokes. You lack the brainless certainties that allow uncomplicated intercourse, and this often causes disillusionment in Libran Sloane sex. Your sense of curiosity keeps you on the outside, watching, and Sloane men become nervous. There is a critical, argumentative element which makes you difficult, unpredictable. You are easily bored, and need the stimulation of new arguments, or the same arguments with new people. Socially you are completely promiscuous, but a natural sense of snobbery confines liaisons to the upper middle classes. Your low threshold may lead you into eccentric dressing habits – you look particularly attractive in a man's shirt and tie, his waistcoat, his cufflinks and stiff collars. Sloanes on the way out may appear in a wet 'n' stretchy one-piece rubberwear, but you are less successful as a leather mistress ('I feel *sooooo* silly I can't tell you!') Despite your large vocabulary, and larger than necessary body, you don't have much to say in sexual matters. You are too keen for conversation, and you gossip too much to enjoy being the subject of gossip. So you feel left out of the action during sex, as though bored by a man's obsessive monologue, going on and on repeating himseif. If he scoops your legs up over his shoulders and bears down on you you look at him with curiosity: 'Why are you doing that?' you ask. And when detumescence sets in: 'You aren't going to sleep, are you?' you say warningly. You may even argue about it, but as you won't fight, you lose. You undress carefully and stand in your slip scrubbing little stains out of your shirt, chatting lightly about Venetian glass. Your attitude to sex is sensible, and you don't always prevent his hands moving into restricted areas. Sex for you is an extension of dancing ('Nothing beats a good bop') and your rhythmic variations will surprise your partners, no less than your footwork. Men often fall out, but you never stop moving to the music, and your hands flutter across his back. He may make the mistake of thinking you are joining in, and some disappointment may result when he finds you are hand-jiving. Your larger than average breasts, and your greater than average drinking, cushion you against inconsiderate body weight.

yet been to bed with her conventionally – pay no attention).

These phrases will help you while meeting the parents:

1 'Sir' (as in 'Couldn't agree more, Sir').
2 'Well of course she is going a bit barmy, but *someone* had to break the miners.'
3 'But imagine actually having to *live* in America! I rest my case!'
4 'Do you know, Mrs Buchanan, when you were coming through the orchard I honestly thought you were Fanny!'
5 'Well, in my view the pendulum is swinging away from promiscuity and stage nudity, and it can't swing too quickly in my view. I hope I'm not offending anybody?'

GROUP SEX

This rarest of Sloane phenomena has been noted only at the Lots Road auction sales (21 Lots Road, SW6, 6.30 every Monday). The isolated practice of Sloane 'swinging' may be observed as contacts are made for sexual purposes between rogue Sloanes who have not been introduced. Offers are made through the bidding system (lots 69, 96 and 369 are the trigger signals) and couples pair up outside. It also explains the price achieved by the deeply depressing mahogany furniture which they buy there.

HOMOSEXUALITY

This technique of pair/peer bonding, used in basic training of specialist army cadres, is traditionally more common in male public schools, though detailed research shows that, indeed, convent girls are at it like knives.

The odour of homosexuality forms an integral part of the traditional atmosphere of public schools, so integral that it is only subliminally noticed by Sloanes. Grammar school girls, however, reel back from it clutching their throats and making gagging noises.

The leading public schools may be ranked:

Winchester. Ask around the European history section of the library for Susie. Gunner's Hole is the favoured rendezvous, around midnight on hot summer nights.

Eton, Windsor, Berkshire. Ages thirteen to eighteen. Contact Bunty in the old library for introductions.

Marlborough, Marlborough, Wiltshire. Ages thirteen to eighteen. Contact 'The Right Rev' Lulu (fifteen in November).

Ampleforth, York, North Yorkshire. Catholic single-sex offers greatest opportunities, contact the Venerable Squashee-Bottom (or Binky).

Rugby Warwickshire. No information available at time of press.

Wellington, Crowthorne, Berkshire.

Ever since sexual statistics were first kept (sometime in the late fourteenth century) Wykehamists have spent a substantial proportion of their leisure and recreational timetable diddling one another senseless. They have suffered little from society, as politicians, law lords, merchant princes and senior dukes will testify – as indeed they do testify, when called upon by the High Court as character witnesses for their colleagues. It is described, on oath, as significant as blowing your nose ('Don't want to go round with a runny nose').

The utility of this form of intercourse is high: the effect on later careers is beneficial

SCORPIO

As the most darkly ambitious of the Sloane Zodiac you present a great threat to lighter signs. Your purpose is to rattle your opposition, and your sexual activities (you're interested in sex in a perfectly un-Sloane way) have precisely this effect. There is an engine in your body which generates intensity and pain. You are awkward socially and feel, correctly, that you don't fit in. Feeling you have to tell the truth, your small talk is appallingly inflated – love and death, religion and politics ('Can't be bothered with trivial, meaningless yapping,' both men and women say), and whole parties can recoil from you, leaving you glaring at them from a corner ('Bit intense, that one'). Your dinner conversation produces a mêlée of indignant stupidity. As a result you may be more than usually deprived in your sexual experiences, and in the Sloane world this is saying something. Experience encourages you to moderate your behaviour, but you can never quite eliminate the smoulder in the back of your eyes. In bed you rear back, nostrils flaring, and the whites of your eyes flashing danger signals. You grip men in a coil of sex, and squeeze them wickedly, you strike in deep with your sting, down into the soft parts of their secret places ('Steady, I say, *steady!*'). There is no post-coital peace for you, and after the act you lie back on your side, working your eyes at your partner ('Anything wrong old girl?'). They think you suffer from foreign blood, probably Lebanese. Notwithstanding this you can have almost anyone you want at least once, and sometimes twice. You give them so much that they don't have to come back for a year, and they leave hastily ('Whew!'). You do things to them in bed which no true Sloane would do – which no true Sloane even *knows* about. However these sexual problems pale beside your performance in discos. Your authentic dance style is unsuitable for anything outside an ethnic festival. For this reason you find difficulty maintaining Sloane liaisons (word gets around), and you either turn to sexual heavyweights in the boxing world, or you sublimate your drive into trying to penetrate the House of Lords. The other problem is that you are not susceptible to Sloane perversions (they have a formal, scripted element to them, and this is important as everyone needs to know where they are), but you can suddenly lash out with some spontaneous demand that will make an insubstantial banker shake. It all leads to complicated relationships as your aggressive attitude to simple Sloane men suggests that, like Aries, you are looking for someone to take care of you. Though you frequently live below the sexual poverty line (resources in the Sloane environment are at Third World levels) you are quite capable of taking care of yourself, and sympathy makes you angry. But your social ambitions, as intense as your sexual, bind you to the world of pearls and green gumboots, unsatisfactory as you find it in many respects. Others should remember you will not forgive or forget, however you disguise your nature. Your husband's inability to provide a listed country house in Gloucestershire eliminates any respect you may have had for him very early on, and your implacable resentment eats away at you both. Once thinking to cheer you up, he tried to take you roughly from behind in the kitchen. You killed him.

and connections established here lubricate the entry to a good merchant bank after university. However, the homosexuality of this Sloane freemasonry is not purely formal and participation is expected throughout the career ('All hands to the pumps'), particularly at lunches celebrating a signing. The practice was instrumental through the oil crises in retaining Arab money in the City, and accounts for approximately fifteen billion sterling in foreign currency reserves (though younger bankers often experience lung trouble after signing a large loan).

Though Winchester leads the statistics on quantity, the worldliness of Etonians takes the prize for quality. Homosexual operations at that school have historically taken on an international character and generate a positive balance of payments for the school in the allocation of preferred shares in public company floats.

Sloane women discontinue the practice after school and 'drop their cracks'* ('It's just for kids').

In both sexes it is generally (71 per cent, Hayling poll, 1982) found to be impossible to duplicate the intensity of emotional excitement in any subsequent, post-educational environment. 'My face used to go red' (82 per cent), 'At sixteen I used to blush like a teenager' (64 per cent). 'If Vicki Patterson didn't wear the Cock House pin I gave him on his lapel I knew something was terribly wrong. He didn't speak to me for days sometimes, even though I was Captain of the XXX. It became a battle of wills. When I finally approached him after Big School he just broke into a great smile and said 'Sorry Dray, I didn't think you cared any more', and turned his lapel over – the pin had been there all the time! That night I cried. It was the last time I ever cried' (56 per cent).

*Crack – a junior admirer, West Heath slang, equivalent to *lush, tutsy, blue-boy, smiley, pattacake, welly, flooze, scum, pook, punk*, and *pash-pal*.

AUTO-EROTICISM

This practice does not feature significantly amongst female Sloanes. As the function of sex is to expand the net of social contacts there is no purpose in self-abuse. However, with Sloane men the practice is endemic, as they find partners so hard to come by (they have problems with their mothers and their housemasters). Since the crises in sterling, Sloane men use the by-product of this activity to rag the walls of their flats in Parson's Green.

EXHIBITIONISM

The only occasions on which Sloane women are subject to attacks of compulsive self-abuse are when they are extending their property. Here the excitement of tax-free capital gain, combined with the envy of non-banking neighbours, make the two-bedroomed loft conversion a powerful focus of social progress. This triggers the sexual impulse, and builders may often surprise (though not embarrass) Sloane wives lowering themselves on to hammer handles, rolling pins, paint brushes ('Would you mind knocking in future, please, *thank you*').

All normally developed Sloanes will take their clothes off, when drunk, to go swimming. The cleft of many Sloane buttocks can be closely defined by their flesh hugging polka-dot pants. At private houseparties over the weekend Sloanes will occasionally come down for dinner dressed only in Mummy's tiara. This should not be taken as a weakness for sensuality. There is nothing indulgent or voluptuous in Sloane exhibitionism. Its purpose is to amuse. Overheated reaction betrays an alien presence and results in his social disappearance from the group.

SAGITTARIUS

You are most often seen in a dinner jacket, describing an arc into a swimming pool – you rarely wait to be thrown by others. This ebullient, deeply boring sign is traditionally that of Sloane men ('Polish m'rocket, there's a good girl'), but both sexes enjoy a sportive attitude to sex, it's a co-operative recreation, somewhere between playing tennis and making mudpies – you do it for the exercise. Both sexes throw up more than any other sign: 'Driving the porcelain bus,' you say, and 'Talking to the big white telephone.' It is surprising you are so popular. Female Sloanes born under this sign suffer from a party-girl reputation and range over the countryside killing things. Men think you are great ('Triffic girl') and you can even get romantic yourself in a porky sort of way. Your sense of snobbery is concealed beneath a universal bonhomie (you're *fright*fully good with servants) and you have half a dozen things you can say to anyone in the world, by which time you're old friends. You are often seen astride a man's shoulders (he has his head up your dress) fighting another mounted girl, making a great deal of noise. You careen into strangers, and having drunk too much, everything goes dark. You awake as from a dream upside down on your shoulders, pedalling the air, with some appalling sort of man groaning between your thighs ('My *God!* Who are *you!*' you suddenly say, introducing the note of confusion into the proceedings for which you are famous). However your steeple chasing abilities are impressive – ranging across the social landscape in pursuit of the perfect drinks party, the smartest dinner party, the most boisterous weekend in the country. You are immensely popular in big houses where the presence of children has put all breakables out of reach. Men quickly become overheated when they hear you've been asked, as one of them at least will do it with you (unless it's a long weekend). The others know there is a good chance of commandeering you on your way back from his room to yours ('Good idea, I was just getting into my stride'). When enjoying yourself you can throw a man around the bed, but it's more a function of your sense of humour than of sexual communion. Alone in the Sloane Zodiac you can make a great deal of noise – you know all the words to *He Taught me To Yodel, Yodel Odel Dee!* – and you may be appreciative afterwards ('Cor, that wasn't half bad!'). Sex is most clearly social intercourse for the Sagittarian, and you may roar with laughter, and shout progress reports to those in adjoining rooms. More Sagittarians than any other sign are involved in salacious games of charades, midnight raids on guest rooms, forcible stripping of party folk, and scenes of group sex ('Anyone for Denis? *Denis!*'). You will be provided with our cosiest entertainment in bed with a fag and his fagmaster – you hold no grudges (you can't remember to) and men are alternately glad and rather resentful you don't remember who they are and whether you've done it with them or not. You have a cheerfully blundering tongue ('Oh *poo!*' or more frequently, 'Cooo! What a little willy, is that as big as it gets . . . ? Oh never mind, Mister *Sensitive!*') However, for all your cheerfulness you never beg, or groan, or rake your fingernails across his back, except in relation to your dress allowance. You like doing it best in a tack room, so you can talk about it afterwards. Both sexes are provided with sexual organs of remarkable size, which are often bottled after the autopsy.

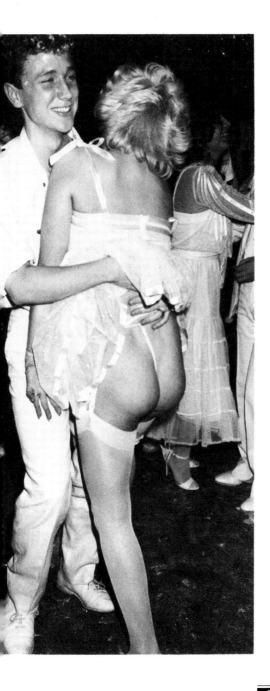

SLUTS

The sub-class of sexually indiscriminate Sloanes (or chalet girls) can be observed running around Val D'Isere looking for trouble but a high proportion of the sub-class come from Guildford and do not have either stabling, grass courts or a long-term commitment to the genus, later undergoing Sloane suicide by forming marital associations with catering managers, journalists, schoolmasters, self-employed electricians ('As long as we're happy, I don't see what's wrong with it.' 'No, I don't suppose you would, darling').

ORAL SEX

'Using her mouth' is an aberration that the genuine Sloane will not countenance ('I think I'm going to be sick, I can't *bear* it, *pleeease*, I hate it *so* much, no *seriously, really* please!').

BEHAVING BADLY

'God we were so drunk last night!'

PIGGY BACKING

feeling in the pit of her stomach, and is the closest that many genuine Sloanes ever come to conventional sexual intercourse. The A.I. scheme is improving the bloodline scientifically.

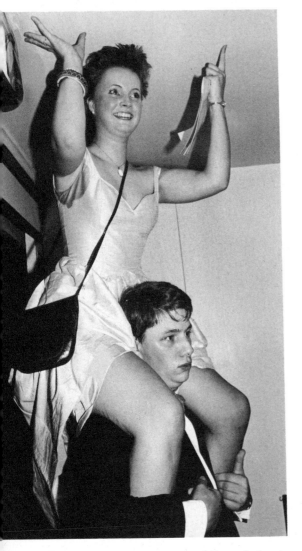

Early experiences with saddlery help to organize Sloane expectations in later life. This activity is obscurely connected with a warm

DANCING

CAPRICORN

Your procreative attitude to sex, and the powerful social ambitions you have harboured since puberty make you a key sign; but your genuine shock at hearing about living lesbian tableaux at Bullingdon dinners suggests your Sloane reactions are confined by middle-class instincts. And the waste distresses you, and the reckless defecation in other peoples' houses. If it weren't for the garden parties, and the value of Queen Anne houses, you would feature less in this world and more amongst the non-denominational professionals. You are impenetrable to Rude Boys. Their casual approaches you find insulting, and you will not be insulted. You have a sharp tongue, and it is well practised: 'What do you think of this?' Rudes will ask, exposing themselves. 'It looks like a penis, only smaller,' you say coolly. Your cautious contempt for Sloane men earns you their deepest affections ('Keeps me in my place, and God knows I need it!'). You find single life vapid and unsatisfactory, and your inviolable air on the sofa makes contact difficult; you sit on your feet for protection, refuse offers of drink (or worse), and when it comes to the moment of decision you only ask 'Is this wise?' Successful men have spent £45 for dinner and move in without doubt or hesitation. They scarcely realize that by performing the act they are contracting a powerful debt themselves, and that you will send out invoices, reminders and final demands – 'Is this wise?' is a pertinent question. You are cool during the act; when he asks you to do certain things you say, 'But why?' You may clear your throat casually during his crisis, you may blow your nose, ('Sorry, couldn't breathe, you know that awful feeling around your sinuses, like a scab? What have you stopped for?') You insist on sex with the light off, and this is just as well, considering the faces of distaste you pull in the dark. Your first experience of sex was disappointing enough to constitute a trauma ('It hurt, rather, if you really want to know') and many of you Capricorn Sloanes carry this bur-den in addition to all the other sexual disabilities of the class. Not that you have to carry it for long – relations are discontinued after the fifth child. Such is your flinty nature that your friends are surprised how easily you marry – you marry earliest of any Sloane sign ('You may think I'm old-fashioned, and I'm sorry for it, but I can't apologise'). Middle age comes to you early (about twenty-four), but your active interest in the share market keeps senility off for longer than any other Sloane sign. There is something deeply reassuring in your implacable nature, and you step easily into that part of the Sloane man's heart which his housemaster has just vacated. If married to an obsessive Sloane man you may consent to whip him ('Darling you've no idea how silly you look'), but you will barter this against his demands for intercourse ('It's *very* difficult to respect a man once one's seen him in "that" position'). Also the general sense of contempt you feel for men ('Such *little* boys') is reinforced by the practice. Notwithstanding, you begin a family at once, and with your Victorian values the family is a large one. As a sound and serious social entrepeneur you provide a beautiful home and discipline for the children and your husband, who may be driven to drink because of it. The discipline of separate bedrooms from an early stage helps preserve the mystery of marriage (the mystery is how your husband puts up with it). You never talk about sex except in an agricultural context, but you often deal in pints of bulls' semen. You signal your availability for intercourse by leaving a jar of Nivea outside your room on Saturday night. It may take your husband years to recognize the significance of the Nivea (or perhaps he doesn't want to realize it – he suffered a very bloody nose after you'd only been married nine months. 'Just popping in to see if you're all right,' and you savaged him; 'Of *course* I'm all right, what makes you think I'm not *all right?* What have I done *now?*').

PARTY NUDITY

(see p. 99)

SLOANE COUNTRY DIARY

Such an embarrassing visit to gynae – remembered too late H's attentions night before and doctor v. curious to know how marks got on my bottom. Quick thinking me – 'Sitting on a grating' (!). Dubious look on his university face. 'I'd be more careful in future.' Oh woe! Got to cut down on the alcohol. Tried to talk to H. about it, got stupidly upset. He tried to calm me down and in struggle bumped heads – luckily scarf hides bruise on side of face, but can't go to Foleys' dance in town, hey ho. H. v. understanding about it, such a poppet, he'll have to take Melissa I'm afraid, hope it won't be too dreary. H. gets so angry at spending money on Sophie's layette, I'm making it all myself on the wind-up Singer we found in the cellar, the clothes look a bit funny, but warm. Poor H. they took his licence away. The robins are singing, and lots of heavenly blue flowers in the water meadows. Must find out their names for Sophie. *Glorious* colours. Ate a caterpillar in a salad by mistake (yuck!). Haven't had any house-guests for too long, must make an effort. *Must* get some beds.

H. spoke to me today. Checking diary it's the first time for six weeks. Hope he's all right. Too hot for tennis lesson (and too poor). Doesn't seem like autumn. Man came to cut down box tree, put in flower beds on first terrace. Tried to clear nettlebeds by self, got frightfully stung, hope Sophie won't mind. (She *won't* mind, will she?) Glorious Indian summer – very hot and smelly – this is what causes H. to speak though cannot make out the words. Dreadfully hot nights under a sheet – and no nightie! Touch H. accidentally and he moves over to extreme edge of bed (pig, he says I'm *sooooo* fat). 'September blows soft til the fruit's in the loft.'

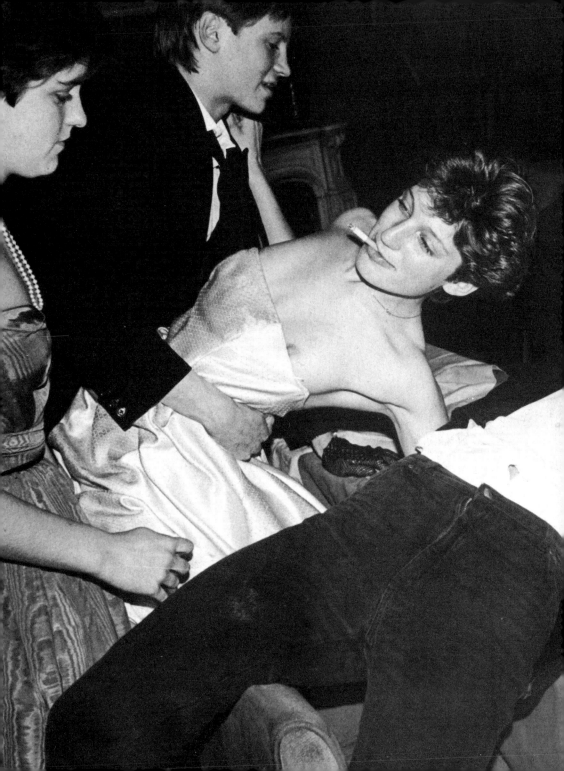

SLOANE COUNTRY DIARY

Told the sister the contractions were coming at the right intervals and she said not to be a fusspot it wasn't nearly time. Eventually had to call gynae myself on public telephone outside ward – he was furious, middle of the night. Couldn't come as H. hadn't settled any of his accounts. Shame H. couldn't have been there for Sophie's arrival. Wonder where he is. I hope he likes my little lamb (hope *I* do too), men are so funny. A*b*solutely *wrung*. Sophie rather funny looking, but clean bill of health from *nice* Asian doctor. But oh dear, how painful breast feeding is. Saw a sparrow and several pigeons on hospital lawn, and many daffodils in vase on next woman's table.

Conkers all over the lawn, crisp autumn morning, it's Sophie's first day home, I don't think I've slept for three weeks. She *cries* continually, I hope I'm doing everything right, *do* try. H. back at last, had been staying with Melissa but lost the piece of paper with name of hospital on it (*so* hopeless). Wish Mummy could come and help but she gets on so badly with H. I can't tell who's Red Rag and who's Bull. *Must* arrange godmothers – should be local? Perhaps Mrs Wilson? Last of the summer birds flying away south. I walk with wailing baby around garden. H. absorbed with mini-computer game. The obs. nob said he'd put a couple of extra stitches in after the episiotomy – I don't suppose he need have bothered, H. says I'm too fat (it's true). A dwarf was murdered in next village by an angry husband (*aren't* people peculiar?)

AQUARIUS

Because you want everyone to *like* you (your Sloane-sense values friendship more than anything) you are able to defuse many potentially sexual situations with earnest talk and wild assertions. Sloane men find this interesting but hard work, and after a couple of dates move on to some more predictable slut. You are demanding, and what you demand (an open invitation to his family house and indissoluble friendship) is the one thing they are most reluctant to give. Luckily you do not suffer from jealousy. You give the impression of a wild and entertaining girl, and you have that social talent to come crashing through social barriers with what looks like a sexual intensity. However you need lavish displays of affection and loyalty (you will act very badly to test loyalty), interspersed with passages of pleasant contempt. You are passionate about everything except your love-life where you can be surprisingly shy for such a big mouth. This equips you perfectly for the Sloane world, and you react favourably at first to the strange disciplines (so batty are you that formal codes impress you with their authority and coherence). However, you have great difficulty keeping it up, and your authentic nature bursts through, embarrassingly, like a raucous fart at a wedding. Your mind is so scattered by ideas, ideals and protestations of friendship that you have difficulty keeping contact with your actual self, placing an exaggerated importance on what your mother thinks – one of the most Sloane characteristics. This is not immediately obvious as your vigorous expression leads many to think you to be forceful and independent. Sexually it seems you are trying to make contact with your inner nature, using your partner as a cross between a psychiatrist and a vibrator, neither of which advances your ambitions in the Sloane world ('Trick cyclists and fancy equipment, oh *God!*'). You talk a lot in bed, not about 'it' but about gypsies, and thatchers, fairness and democracy, freedom and friendship, and the important relationship between them all. Sloane men don't like talking in bed at all, but this couldn't be worse. Used to nervous girls though they are, this is unacceptable. When he tries to stop your mouth you gag. Drawn to the eccentric as you are, your partners will either be unsuitable socially, or incompetent sexually. You suffer from a divided life until you meet such a combination of birth and continental education that you abdicate all personal responsibility (thereby losing him at once). You are not susceptible to Rude Boys – any further unpredictability in your world would seriously destabilize your already unstable personality. Your lack of contact with your physical nature can lead to awkwardness and embarrassment, something quite alien to the Sloane persona. And once it is detected your Sloane days are numbered.

MOILING IN THE MIDDLE OF THE ROOM

Sloanes are socially self-employed, at the level of plumbers and electricians. They lack the uncompetitive camaraderie of less ambitious social units. Bristling with signals and ambition, it is difficult to get close to them, and perhaps it's just as well.

However, the series of self-contained units has a political vitality, but a sense of personal isolation (see *The Communist Manifesto*, Marx and Engels). So we see Sloanes, lubricated by a sense of class solidarity, getting as close as they can while remaining on the outside of each other. Reliving the lost intensity of public school intimacy – something not sexual, but a deeply passionate *weltschmerz* experience (like lacrosse).

Moiling is a fine example of Sloane body language and strictly translates as 'I am lonely'.

MEN PUNCHING EACH OTHER

The crisp exchange of views is central to Sloane life, and conversation rattles like a bilateral printer. The fight that has developed is the signal that it is time to go home.

THE BULLINGDON

Middle-class attitudes are hostile to this most prestigious of Oxford dining clubs, and this is a major defence in the social structure of Sloane solidarity ('It may seem extraordinary

SLOANE COUNTRY DIARY

H. has Mrs Wilson back to help with the house (I can't cope, but what a surly woman she is, and her *breath*!). I'm sure she takes her wages over again in drink from our cellar. But happy day! Melissa arrived for a week, such fun to see a proper face. H. rather ungracious, but she's probably used to him. We go out and tour the property, eat wild pears, explore the potting sheds, and stroll in the copse. *Such* a glamorous life she's leading, it makes me feel quite rustic. The back of the manor thick with wisteria and looks 'deeply moving' according to M. Wake H. for dinner. Bindy brought in a bat to the kitchen by its wing, and killed it, *so* horrid, I was sick.

H. wants to teach me self defence, but he's so rough. I get the feeling he doesn't love me very much at the moment. And really I don't *really* need to know how to box. Poor sinners in Norfolk aren't really violent. I'm probably a bear of *very* little brain, H. knows best about these things. Buy track suit and *enormous* boxing gloves. Where is H.?

Not having seen H. for twelve days I did what I promised I'd never do. I went through his papers. He lost his job with Barings seven months ago, and has been living on supplementary benefit, and my savings. He has taken a job as sales director with a double glazing firm in Ilford. Also, something he hasn't told me is that the Council has asked to buy the garden up to the kitchen wall to build a by-pass, and even though they couldn't get a compulsory purchase order Henry has agreed. I have drunk a bottle of brandy and taken a very large number of sleeping pills. Who will feed Sophie, I'm just too tired. Where is H.? He should have been home hours ago.

Behind the closed doors of a Keats Society Dinner, traditional values reassert themselves. Truth and beauty predominate. 'It's just a phase.'

to *you*, but *you* weren't there, so I don't see how you're in a position to judge – it's actually perfectly innocent fun').

After dinner entertainment traditionally begins with a living lesbian tableau comprising three black girls who climb on to the table and lap at one another's genitals like labradors. Bullingdon members, wearing white tie and the distinctive velvet-collared tailcoats, fire champagne corks between the girls' legs at a distance of twenty-five feet. The girls attempt to catch the corks and fire them back again. The lack of black girls on the Buller membership list causes the club to buy girls in from the town. The occasion concludes by driving naked or semi-naked Sloanes down the Great West road in open cars shooting out stop lights at all intersections with twelve-bores.

PISCES

A streak of subordination makes you attractive to Sloane men, though Sloane women find you rather hopeless, and silly, and indiscriminate. Your sexually responsive nature has been cruelly perverted in the Sloane matrix of response and non-response, and you are confused as a result. In your early days you were inclined to do it with some intelligence, but a hostile reaction has reorganized your ideas. With Gemini you make up the bulk of the Sloane sluts. Motivated men ravish you on a pile of coats at drinks parties, Rude Boys surround you in restaurants and breathe into both your ears at once, desperately oversexed Sloane perverts (usually aged over forty) tie your knees to the back of your neck and effect multiple penetration. You smile occasionally, and look out of the window. During the act you drift away on some private tide, your eye on a horizon invisible to anyone else. You react to sexual abuse better than any other sign in the Sloane Zodiac, but find it hard to form enduring relationships, especially when your Piscean nature dominates the Sloane. However, the two may come together occasionally, and it will constitute the only satisfactory Sloane knowledge of sex, experienced through an ideal of submission, shame and strange independence. 'Call me a slut!' you whisper fiercely, and it will unsettle the inexperienced man. 'You are a slut?' he may say nervously, and will react badly to the rest of the sequence: 'What kind of slut? A filthy slut? What do you do to filthy sluts? Tell me what you should do to me!' Men find you fairly impossible (you fail to turn up to dinner parties, you're never ready on time, you call men by the wrong name, you fake orgasms and they are absurdly theatrical, or worse, you are so removed from the experience you don't bother faking them at all). Post-coitally you may often be seen in a man's shirt, bending over the hotplate, fixing a bacon sandwich, fetching a can of beer from the fridge, and this makes your many partners long to see you again. However, only Princes can get really close to Pisceans, and even they can't. You are too dreamy to react sharply enough to the Sloane world and you find a lot of the dress code burdensome. When you go into piggy back fights you lose. Such ambition as you have could fit into a cokespoon. But you don't mind pleasing others, and will assume a variety of humiliating positions to increase your popularity. You may, if pushed by an experienced hand, allow yourself to share a bed with another girl. You will permit intercourse in a variety of peculiar places (physical and geographical) but you object to whipping ('It *hurts*!'). You can also be sarcastic. This more than anything makes you drop like a stone out of Sloane society.

been in happier times a traditional forum for public nudity, and titled women checked all their clothes at the door to enjoy dancing and drinks wearing only pearls, heels and handbag. This did not constitute exhibitionism (q.v.) in anthropological terms, but fancy dress. Comments included 1) 'There's nothing as unsexy as a completely naked woman', 2) 'Thank God the men don't do it as well', and 3) 'God, Clarissa's got a lot of pubic hair'. Times have, sadly, changed, and now pleasant old folk enjoy themselves, as we see pictured. This may be a relic of flagellational submission, an attack of exhibitionism, or guests showing their opinion of photographers at Sloane parties.

PARTY NUDITY

Sloane men may produce a *membrum virile* (often not their own) and lay it on a plate of cold cuts, to be offered around with drinks. Sloane women squeal, 'Put it away!' (Senior men agree and say 'Where? Hahaha!')

The practice fulfills the function of peer-bonding, and Sloanes cheerfully spear the member with a toothpick ('Sorry! Thought it was a cocktail sausage!') The same men earn the right (a debased variant of the *droit de seigneur*) of stripping a chosen Sloane to the waist and applying handfuls of guacamole to her chest for the senior Sloane present to remove with his mouth.

The annual Midsummer's Eve Party at the Arts Club in Dover Street (invitation only) has

This girl is unlikely, in fact, to be a Sloane, but she has a remarkably attractive figure, and she conforms to the Sloane discipline of backward display, offering excitement without responsibility.

Though the wine has not yet arrived, things are getting under way. This is not, of course, an invitation, or even a challenge. 'A sense of humour is frightfully important.'

SEXUAL
FANTASIES

PALACE

In a recent research probe this fantasy scored highest amongst suburban Sloanes – 38 per cent finding it 'frightfully arousing' – and throughout the Home Counties as far out as Aylesbury and Godalming, though falling off in Kent – 12 per cent finding it 'really rather arousing' – and the Buckinghamshire borders – 'not particularly arousing actually'.

'I don't know who he is at the Spastics Charity Ball, but he keeps asking me to dance. Hugo, who I'm with, gets pretty terrifically annoyed actually (his family lives in the Brecon Beacons where the SAS train) but he can't say anything because he *does* know who this guy is (he might have *told* me!) so he just gets awfully drunk and strange, and I go on dancing with what I think is just this rather good looking *guy*. Anyway, eventually he has to take me home because Hugo's just hog-whimpering, and outside on the doorstep he kisses me, and I don't stop him for a while because it's actually rather nice, because he doesn't do it greedily (like Jamie) or feebly (like Mot), or messily like Hugo does (honestly Hugo's *so* disgusting, he's got this *huuuuuge* tongue) and he puts his arm around my waist (I've got Mummy's ball dress from the fifties on, it's bare shoulders with a spray of pink taffeta and enormously flared skirt, she's never let me borrow it before, she hasn't allowed me to borrow anything not since Hugo cleaned his horse with her *Dior scarf* when we were all so ill on the peterpee) and we get into his black Bentley, which is convertible, and we drive out into the Mall at about 3 a.m. on one of those warm mornings, and even though it's so warm I've got goosebumps under the Georgian lace shawl (one of Mummy's granny's, it's been in the family forever) on my shoulders where he touched me, it's actually weird, and he's driving really fast, whooshing along and I can't understand it because we pass really lots of policemen who just salute us as we go past, and this guy just smiles (he's terrifically good looking when he smiles, even though he's not conventionally handsome). Then we turn off the Mall in through these huge wrought iron gates and go into a courtyard which is terrifically old with lots of really ancient doorways leading off under these cloisters, with gaslight just like when Hugo was at Cambridge, and he stops the car outside one of them and turns the engine off. Servants in knee breeches look on from the shadows. He turns to me in the front seat, and slides over the bench seat. His dinner jacket really is brilliant. He puts his face close to mine. He says something suggestive. I reply, quite well. But then he puts his hand somewhere and I hold his wrist to stop him and the light catches his cufflinks which have a really deep inner glow of incredible ancientness and wealth. His breath comes faster. He struggles with the taffeta, and tries to push his hand with a really fine signet ring into my pretty bra. But I just smile sadly because it cannot be, I hardly know who he is.'

SLOANE MASOCHISTIC FANTASY

Exposure to this scenario commonly induces symptoms of extraordinary stress in 100 per cent of Sloanes questioned, including accelerated heart-rate, sweating in palms, and a radial flush from the aural lobes downwards. The signals were indistinguishable from major sexual arousal, though this was repeatedly, even hysterically denied.

'He picked me up in a *wine bar*. Gosh and Dots thought I was joking. Daddy won't speak to me. Mummy speaks to me but she doesn't smile any more. He's got a moustache. And he wears a bracelet with a strip of metal which has his *name* on it. He taps his cigarette ash off with his middle finger. His shirts are made of permapress acrylic, and there's a terrible sour smell under his chin of scent, and bad breath and fast food. He's a sales director for a chain of laundromats. He takes me to 'the pictures'. He puts his arm around me in the back row. His hand in my lap is like a small animal. He rubs his wet rubbery lips all over my face. He pays for dinner with an Access card. He takes me back to the place he calls his pad. He says 'Come on darling, you know you love it.' I tell him how revolting he is, that I find him disgusting, that I'm leaving immediately. He grabs me clumsily and pushes me against his microwave and rubs his lips all over my face again. His saliva leaves snail tracks on my cheeks and they smell of dogs. He turns me round and pushes my head into the sink where the washing-up and the cabbage water is, by the nape of my neck. He pulls up my clothes. He tears my underwear. He does unspeakable things. He uses the Fairy Liquid. He uses the cake slice. Then he makes himself a cheese sandwich and watches video highlights of *Match Of The Day*. I am unable to leave. Where would I go? Who would touch me now? My work deteriorates and I lose my job at Christie's. He waits for me outside and takes me back to Wimbledon and abuses me with household appliances. I have two children by him and he calls both of them Wayne. They go to minor public schools, and one is arrested for shoplifting and the other gets a qualification from a technical college. My husband achieves office in the Council. My best friend is called Tina. When I see Mummy in town, on my birthday, I thank her everso for her prezzie. But she gets up from the table suddenly, without looking at me, I think she's crying and I never see her ever again when she hears me saying, 'Excuse me garçon, can you tell me, do you have a toilet here?'

GEORGIAN HOUSE

This scenario stimulates a sexual flush, dilated pupils and positive sexual lubrication in 85 per cent of Sloanes. Symptoms were monitored electronically by EEG, in 40 per cent of the cases. The other 45 per cent made a dive for the researchers' trouser buttons.

'It's rather noisy, actually, in this fantasy – it's the noise of summer evening insects. There are woodcock too, in a screen of dark beeches. There's a single tall Scotch Pine which is the one stark note in our Gloucestershire garden. Mrs Wilson-Without-Whom-We-Couldn't-Do is taking in the tea things by the kitchen door. There is honeysuckle, and a shy dog and a little girl up past bedtime. On the hillsides the sheep don't sound like sheep (baa baa!) but go ohhh! errr! urgghh! like peasants greeting each other, complaining, in pain, poor peasants. The listed Georgian hall is faced with Cotswold stone, and you step out under the tall sash window straight on to the two-hundred-year old lawn, where the grass grows as fine as hair. The little girl runs pell-mell in a blue frock across the croquet lawn, in front of the grass courts. The rolling sheep-filled hills will never be yours. They'll be your cousin Jamie's, it's so unfair because he was born after you, but it doesn't matter in this summer evening, because here comes Daddy in his flannels, home from the village cricket on this perfect summer evening.'

ART DEALER

This was the least nominated scenario, 35 per cent finding it 'actually distasteful', and 45 per cent finding it 'stupid'.

'I find myself flirting with a Roman art dealer at a party. He touches me gently at the back of the neck and asks me why I'm so sad. This is clever of him as I've been talking and laughing 'til my throat's sore. In his flat where we suddenly find ourselves something happens, but I can't seem to say what it is. There are tapestries on the wall, and an oriental bird chained to a perch, and it says things. There are large pieces of furniture where we sit, or lie, or roll over. He says things, when he has to. I feel light-headed, perhaps he has given me drugs. But though I can't describe what I see, I see everything. But it has a sort of light inside it which pulses, then crackles; when I draw my fingers across his chest there are sparks. It is not love between us but an unbearable excitement at this contact. There is pleasure too, and it begins in my kidneys, pumping in a stream up through the spine, over my shoulders and into my heart. Every time he looks at me, or says something there is another rush. This must be what men feel in their sex, but it happens all through my back, and chest and heart. It makes me think I will never die.'

EIGHTS WEEK

Scenario most favoured by the genus pseudo-Sloane, 65 per cent from Guildford and Dorking whose fathers work in insurance companies or high street banking.

'We meet up in London with Gosh and Atty in Beaufort Street, and they introduce me to the person who is going to drive us up to Oxford for the last day of Eights Week (I'm terrified because I won't know a soul, and Daddy's only a barrister). And he's *divine*, called the Hon. Edmund Grevesney, and it turns out he knows practically everyone *I* know. Gosh drives the Bentley and Edmund and I sink into the back bench seat by ourselves, the car's so big, the back's like a sofa and it's very discreet, terribly private, no-one can see us at all. He brushes my leg as he pours champagne. It turns out he spent the weekend with Amanda and Lucie and Dots who were at school with his cousin Maria from Northumberland who's now working at Aspreys with Tish and Sacks who I met skiing last year with Tom and Headley. I feel as if I've known him for ever, and when I tell him this his hand slides up under my pretty summer dress, up past the tops of my stockings to the soft skin at the top of my legs which jumps as he touches it. *Then* it turns out his family used Daddy as a Q.C. when his brother used to share a flat with Houghton and Henry and all those boys from Eton like Renfrew and Postleton who've both joined the Brigade of Guards and Willy Wekes who used to go out with Atty in Battersea when Johnny was working at Barings and I used to come in from Hungerford because I was staying with the Romneys before I moved in with Josef and Jules in the New King's road, just round the corner from where Roddy Llewellyn lived (we used to see him in the pub when Daddy was first given his knighthood). By this time Ed has climbed round in between my legs, and somehow got his trousers round his knees and is pushing aside my panties, and pushing at me with his hard maleness just like at Glyndebourne last year when I was sitting opposite the Jeffreys who Daddy put up for Lloyds which is something you can only do if you're a Baronet like Daddy, and Ed suddenly goes in all the way pushing in with this long gasp in the back of his throat, and he arches his back and pushes up into me on the points of his toes and he goes blue in the face just like Hercules McClaren looked after his divorce from Jennifer who shared a room at the clinic with Lippy Diniver. He puts his hands under my bottom and pulls me to him, and lifts my knees up over his shoulders and sinks deep into me, and I respond, making a mess of the leather upholstery in the back of the Bentley. But so abandoned are we that this is irrelevant. He growls passionately reminding me of Lily my labrador who died when I was eleven when the Lumleys so kindly bought me a pony from the Hungerford Academy the year that Hetty Morrissey married that awful Abraham Levi who was a bank manager, and nobody saw them again after Bunty's party she shared with Muff and old Jamie Dundonald who Daddy knew at Eton before his uncle died and he became a vie! Oh God! a vike! Oh God, oh my God a *viscount!*'

KINDERGARTEN TEACHER

The scenario most favoured by older Sloanes (23–6), and working-class readers of the Daily Mail.

'I look after tiny children at a rather smart kindy in Pimlico. My father is an Earl. I live with tremendously well-bred but inconspicuous girls just by the Little Boltons. I have been going out with a cavalry officer for a year, but I meet a man at a party who owns most of Cornwall and has an amazing flat right in the centre of town. He is looking for a wife, but she has to be a virgin. We get on really well, and his mother likes me. In fact everyone likes me, especially when I get my hair done. We get married on television, and I have such a big dress allowance. Everyone likes me even more, and even though he says I need my bottom smacked I make him get rid of all his friends and have him all to myself whenever I want. And whenever I don't I just dial an aeroplane to take me somewhere else. I have babies and send them to the smart kindy in Pimlico while I spend my dress allowance.'

DRUGS

'I've taken pot twice. The first time it didn't do anything at all and the next time I was sick. I don't know what anyone sees in it, frankly.'

AND ROCK 'N' ROLL

They like Wham! since Cliff Richard got too macho.

PICTURE ACKNOWLEDGEMENTS

Rex Features

p.2 (Richard Young), p.9 and 10 (Herbie Knott), p.11 (The Cleavage), p.12 (Tony Benn), p.15 (Now Lirk! photo by Richard Young), p.19, p.20 (Senior Man), p.22 (The Sloane Bosom), p.23 (The Cheerful Sloane Display), p.24, p.26, p.28, p.33 (by Richard Young), p.35, p.43, p.45, p.54, p.55, p.58, p.70, p.75, p.77, p.85, p.88 (Dancing) p.99 (The Proud Chest – Richard Young), p.101 (Richard Young)

Alpha

p.16 Lady Sarah Armstrong Jones (Alan Davidson), p.17 (Alan Davidson), p.21 (The Perfect Back), p.25 (The Viscount), p.63, p.89, p.96 (Alan Davidson)

Keystone Press

p.20 (Junior Man), p.22 (Girls on the Fence), p.59

Daffyd Jones

p.16 (Sulky Sloane), p.18 (Onanist Dinner), p.21 (Trainee Rude Boy), p.23 (The Perfect Complexion), p.39, p.49, p.50, p.51 (top shot), p.88 (On Shoulders), p.92, p.97

Diana Cochrane

p.99 (Backward Display)

Syndication International

p.12 (The Sloane Hell), p.14 (Topless at Eton), p.18 (Ski Instructor), p.25 (The House), p.31, p.62

Mirror Features

p.25 (The Window), Swaine Adeney Brigg and Sons Ltd, p.27

Central Press Photos

p.11 (The Honeymoon Carriages)

Poppé Folly
The New Astrology £1.95

Everything you've always wanted to know about yourself – but no one dared tell you . . .

Here is the amazing truth about your stars and their influence on practically everything from orgasms to overdrafts, revealed by the astrological *enfant terrible* of the *Tatler*. This unique guide will help you maximize your psychological resources and minimize your traits – whether you've made it, are making it, or just can't get it up. Don't say you haven't been warned . . .